MINI ENCYCLOPEDIA OF
RABBIT
BREEDS & CARE

MINI ENCYCLOPEDIA OF
RABBIT
BREEDS & CARE

A Color Directory Of The Most Popular Breeds And Their Care

Geoff Russell

FIREFLY BOOKS

A FIREFLY BOOK

Published by Firefly Books Ltd. 2009

Copyright © 2009 Interpet Publishing

First printing

Publisher Cataloging-in-Publication Data (U.S.)
Russell, Geoff.
Mini encyclopedia of rabbit breeds and care : a color directory of the most popular breeds and their care / Geoff Russell.
[208] p. : col. photos. ; cm.
Includes index.
Summary: A guide to raising and keeping rabbits. Topics include a history of rabbits, buying and housing rabbits, feeding, health and rabbit shows. Also includes a detailed look at different breeds.
ISBN-13: 978-1-55407-474-7 (pbk.)
ISBN-10: 1-55407-474-6 (pbk.)
1. Rabbits. I. Title.
636.932/2 dc22 SF453.R877 2009

Library and Archives Canada Cataloguing in Publication
Russell, Geoff
Mini encyclopedia of rabbit breeds and care : a color directory of the most popular breeds and their care / Geoff Russell. — 1st ed.
ISBN-13: 978-1-55407-474-7
ISBN-10: 1-55407-474-6
1. Rabbits. 2. Rabbit breeds. 3. Rabbits—Pictorial works.
4. Rabbit breeds—Pictorial works. I. Title.
SF453.R87 2009   636.932'2   C2009-902604-X

Published in the United States by
Firefly Books (U.S.) Inc.
P.O. Box 1338, Ellicott Station
Buffalo, New York 14205

Published in Canada by
Firefly Books Ltd.
66 Leek Crescent
Richmond Hill, Ontario L4B 1H1

Printed in China

This book sets out to provide a complete guide to rabbit breeds and how to maintain a rabbit in good health and happiness for the span of its life. If followed, the program and techniques contained in this book will reap results. Health and safety issues pointed out by the author should be heeded, particularly washing after contact with your pet. It is important, too, to realize that some rabbits are not suitable as children's pets, and the breed section gives advice on this. In all cases of rabbit illness it is advisable to seek the advice of a qualified veterinarian.

The information and recommendations in this book are given without any guarantees on behalf of the author and publishers, who disclaim any liability with the use of this material.

The Author

Geoff Russell was a top breeder and exhibitor of the English Lop breed in Britain for many years. He has also been a British Rabbit Council district advisor and judge.

Russell is well known throughout the rabbit fancy around the world for the numerous magazine articles he has written on rabbit-related topics. He has published three books about rabbits, *A Fancier's Guide to the Lop Rabbit*, *Showing Rabbits* and *The English Lop*. He is probably best known for his long-running monthly column in *Fur and Feather*, which was entitled "Notes from the Shed." Geoff has recently retired from the exhibition-rabbit world and lives with his wife, Lynn, in Cambridgeshire, England.

Contents

PART ONE

Your Rabbit: Getting Started

1 • A Short History

The Domestication of the Rabbit

Early Domestication

The European rabbit is known by the Latin name *cuniculus* (burrower), a name that Linnaeus conferred on it when he published his classifications of flora and fauna in the mid-18th century. Varro (116–27 BCE), the governor of Spain, wrote his treatise on farming entitled *De Re Rustica*, which included a description of the rabbit. He wrote, "Everyone knows, too, that if you put in but a few hares of both sexes, the warren will swarm with them in a short time, so prolific is the quadruped ... often when a litter has not long been born, they are found to have others inside them" and again later, "There is also the recent fashion, now general, of fattening them – by taking them from the warren, shutting them up in cages, and fattening them in confinement." Almost certainly Varro is in fact talking about rabbits rather than hares, as hares are unlikely to "swarm in a short time" or to breed in a warren. And, as we shall see later, it is this start of selective breeding, domestication and fattening in an enclosed environment that would many centuries later produce all the various breeds that we see today.

In his *Natural History*, Pliny the Elder (c. 23–79 CE) tells how, from one pair of escaped rabbits, the Balearic Islands became so infested with wild rabbits, which destroyed the inhabitants' crops and even undermined the houses with their burrows, that the people had to apply to Emperor Augustus of Rome for assistance from his troops to prevent further damage. Pliny records that the troops were sent along with the ferrets to destroy the rabbits.

It is believed that the rabbit actually originated in Spain, or at least in the Iberian Peninsula. But it was the Romans who discovered that rabbits kept in cages could successfully be bred, so that the rabbit became a portable meat (and fur) source for their armies, thus ensuring its distribution throughout the Roman Empire. The cage required to house a rabbit is relatively small, making it ideal for transportation on a ship. One can easily imagine multiple cages of rabbits being kept on the Roman ships to supply the crews and the armies being transported. The early colonizers' journeys were often very lengthy, and the rabbit's short gestation period (30–32 days) would mean the travelers could actually replenish their supplies during the voyage. If this theory is accepted, then it is easy to see how the Romans spread rabbits throughout their dominions. They were equally responsible for the spread of the pheasant, quail and edible door mouse – all things they liked to eat. If the Romans did bring rabbits into England, then they did not survive, probably because of the range of carnivorous predators that roamed the country at that time.

Domestication

The domestication of the wild rabbit almost certainly started in Roman times, with the caging of rabbits. Two opposing theories are

Thetford Warren Lodge

In the middle of many old warrens there stood a single, small building, called the warren lodge. The most famous English lodges were found in the Brecklands of Norfolk, and some date back to the 15th century. The Thetford Lodge had walls over 3 feet (90 cm) thick made of local flint. The roof was thatched and there was a staircase from the ground floor to the second story. The ground floor would have been very gloomy because there was only a single door and window. There were racks for drying rabbit skins and for storing nets and big lanterns for night work. The lodge, standing on the highest part of the warren, was exposed to winds from all directions. The keeper (or warrener) often went to the top of his "lookout" to make sure that his rabbits were in no danger.

put forward as to the evolutionary effects of the caging of rabbits:

- If the caged animals are killed for food and fur, then it is these tamer animals that will continually be eliminated, leaving the wild rabbits to proliferate. Thus caging does not enhance domestication.

- If, as may well have been likely, the caged (and tamer) rabbits lived long and so had more litters, then it is in fact the caged animals that are continually breeding, thus furthering the domestication of the species.

Therefore, caging enhances the development of the domesticated rabbit.

Whichever of these theories you choose to go with, the caging of rabbits has to be considered within the overall picture. Rabbits have been managed by man, and thrived, in a variety of situations for at least the last two millennia: three main systems have been used to rear rabbits for food and their fur:

- Rabbit warrens,
- Rabbit gardens or courts,
- Rabbit islands.

A Warrener

Warrens, or coningrys, were established primarily to protect wild rabbits from carnivorous predators and, in doing so, protect a valuable meat and fur source. Of course, the containment of the rabbits also protected the crops from their destructiveness. Warrens were first noted in England during the Norman period, when the entourage of any self-respecting Norman baron would have a warrener and his ferrets. It was Giraldus, the 12th century Welsh historian, who stated that each feudal lord had his private army, his fishponds and his rabbit warren. At about the same time, and

A warrener or rabbit keeper

for much the same reasons, rabbit warrens were being established in France.

Rabbit warrens

These were fenced or walled areas that allowed the rabbits to burrow into the enclosed mounds and therefore live as "wild rabbits." Some warrens spread over many acres; in fact, large tracts of Norfolk, England, were said to be more profitable under rabbits than cultivation.

Warrens were divided into those from which the rabbits were taken for food and fur and those used to raise rabbits that were then deliberately released into the wild to be hunted for sport. The warrens that kept rabbits for food and fur were a substantial source of income for their owners for many generations. The warrens on the large estates of England that bred rabbits to be released for rough game shooting continued right up until just after the Second World War.

The disease myxomatosis had a devastating effect on the population of wild rabbits in Britain during the 1950s, and although the wild rabbit population has by now all but recovered, many warrens never did.

Rabbit court or garden

The rabbit court was a much smaller affair than the rabbit warren; in a court the rabbits were allowed to run free within an enclosed area while a degree of management was applied to maximize and control the production of stock.

We know from historical records that rabbit courts, probably very similar in many ways to the one described in the facing excerpt, had been employed in monasteries since before the fifth century, and that it was in these courts that

From "The Rabbit Book for the Many"
(*The Journal of Horticulture*, 1867).

I shall take note of something extraordinary relating to a warren, as it was contriv'd and practis'd by the late Lady Belassis at Kensington; her ladyship, among many other curiosities which were cultivated in her gardens, and volaries, disposed one part for the breeding and feeding of Rabbets, in such a manner, as that, by a constant supply of nourishing food, she might draw at any time of the year a sufficient quantity to oblige her friends, and serve her table; but to prevent unsavoury taste which generally attends the flesh of tame Rabbets, consulted as much as possible the nature of the wild sort, how much the open air was beneficial to them, for this end she wall'd in a large square place, and paved it at the bottom, but in some parts had large heaps of earth, ram'd hard, and turf'd, for them to burrow in; but this, which was her first attempt, fail'd, by frequently falling in upon the Rabbets: This however gave her no discouragement; she had a terrass built with arches, and fill'd with earth, leaving proper places for the Rabbets to go in and out; but

still there were many inconveniences, as the falling in of the earth, and males destroying the young ones besides the difficulty of taking them when they are wanted; but at length concluded to build distinct cells for every female, so order'd that they might hide themselves at pleasure, or take the liberty of the enclos'd ground when they thought fit: these cells were cover'd with boards, lying penthouse-wise, made to open at discretion, for the better catching the Rabbets, and to prevent the destroying of does that had young ones: Over the entrance of every cell was a trap-door; either for keeping them in or out: at the south end was a covered place where a couple of buck Rabbets were chain'd for service of the does, and, according to the warreners rule, were enough for twenty-five couples of females: In this place was their food, which was chiefly the refuse of the garden, with some bran and oats, and large blocks of chaulk stone, which they frequently eat to prevent the rot. The pavement or floor was lay'd slopewise for better carrying off the water, and conveniency of cleaning, which was done very often, and contributed greatly to the good thriving of the Rabbets.

selection began to take place, as different colors and mutations occurred. If we want to select a point in history when the domestication of the wild rabbit started, we would almost certainly have to select the papal edict issued by Pope Gregory the Great in 600 CE.

Gregory, the first monk ever to be chosen as pope, decreed that rabbits (or, more correctly, the unborn young or pre-furred young) were not to be classed as a meat and could therefore be eaten by the monks during Lent. This allowed the monks to adopt the

Church pew showing a hare.

Roman habit of eating unborn or newborn rabbits, which were called laurices. The rabbit was an ideal source of protein, and the fur provided warm clothing for the monks in their closed societies. Both of these desirable features were doubtless being selectively bred into the types of rabbit the monks kept. Perhaps one of the other features to be selectively bred was tameness; Darwin (1867) states that "Wild rabbits, if taken young, can be domesticated, though the process is generally troublesome," and one would tend to feel that rabbits bred and raised in an enclosed court would, over numerous successive generations, come to naturally accept people's presence, even if it was only when the human came to feed them. Similarly, one can see that if rabbits kept within a courtyard were able to run away from people, even if not very far away, they would not become domesticated to any extent.

Rabbit islands

Before leaving the early warrens and rabbit courts we must briefly mention the rabbit island, for this was the enclosing of rabbits made easy – no walls, hedges or fences were required. Many of the rabbit islands were very successful, and their history and the effects of isolation on a rabbit population have been the subject of numerous studies (particularly see R.M. Lockley, *The Private Life of the Rabbit, 1954*).

Pens

As we have seen, some kind of cage or pen (or hutch) has been used to confine rabbits since the days of the Phoenicians, who took them on their sea journeys as a self-replacing source of meat and fur; this was a practice continued by the Romans, and almost all the great early colonizers. The development of the rabbit pen, the types of pen required and any special features required will be discussed in some detail later; for now we are only concerned with the effects keeping rabbits in pens had on domestication.

It is almost certainly in the period following Pope Gregory's papal edict of 600 CE that monks, particularly in France, started the process of domesticating the wild rabbit in a combination of rabbit courts and pens.

Almost certainly rabbits were selectively bred

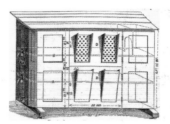

Early rabbit pen, circa 1860.

for size and even color, coat or body shape; keeping them confined in a relatively small area (either a pen or a rabbit court) would no doubt have led to larger animals. By breeding many generations of large rabbits to large rabbits it is feasible to imagine a steady increase in size and weight from the 3-pound (1.4 kg) wild rabbit to the 10,15 or even 20 pounds (4.5–9 kg) of some of the modern breeds. Similarly, the early keepers of rabbits may well have seen genetic mutations appearing in their stock and decided to keep a mutation that appealed to them and thus breed from that mutation into future stock.

There can be little doubt that the enclosing of rabbits in warrens, gardens or courts, islands and pens over the last two thousand years has been responsible not only for the taming of the wild rabbit but also for the characteristics that we recognize the individual breeds by today: size, weight, color, pattern, body type, fur properties, character and eating habits.

A Blue Rex – a medium-sized rabbit.

Netherland Dwarf – a small rabbit.

We have all heard the slogan "a dog is for life, not just for Christmas"; obviously this applies equally to rabbits. They are a 365 days a year commitment; they must be fed and watered, and as social animals they need regular companionship. They must be kept in a secure environment, protected against outside dangers and contained to prevent them from escaping. You must ask yourself if your lifestyle is ready to accept another member of the family and give it the time and affection it deserves.

When buying a rabbit you must make some big decisions before you even approach a pet store or rabbit breeder. Firstly you must decide which breed will best suit your lifestyle. There is a vast difference between a Holland Lop that will only weigh about 3½ pounds (1.6 kg) at adulthood and a Continental Giant that may well have an adult weight of about 20 pounds (9 kg). If you want to show your rabbit then you should visit some shows (see www.arba.net for shows in your area) and look at the different breeds so you know what the alternatives are; it is there that you can talk to exhibitors and breeders. You will find that the vast majority of breeders will be only too happy to speak to you about their breed.

What sex of rabbit do you want? If you intend to keep your rabbit as a pet then you must consider the physical and temperamental differences. Generally speaking, bucks make better pets as they are usually more playful and have more character. The downside of a pet buck is that some become "sprayers" as they mature sexually, and this can be quite pleasant,

Talk to exhibitors and breeders at local shows so that you know what the alternatives are before you choose your rabbit.

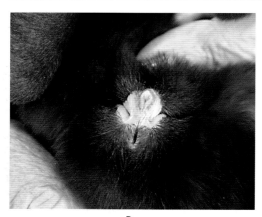

Doe

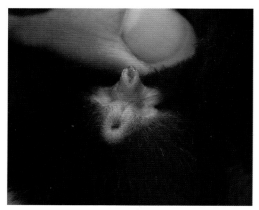

Buck

especially if it is a child's pet. However, having the buck castrated can usually stop him spraying. While many a doe will grow into an affectionate adult, there will be times when she will become quite grumpy and start nest building; it is not uncommon for them to bite the hand that feeds them at this time. It is in every doe's nature to produce young, and if you do not intend breeding from her then it is perhaps best that you have her neutered (make sure that you use a veterinary surgeon who is experienced in rabbit surgery) or buy a buck rather than a doe.

If you intend to show your rabbit, then you should be aware that, generally speaking, only buck lops and fancy rabbits are shown as adults (fur and rex adult does are shown); either bucks or does may be shown in the young stock category, which is under five months of age in most breeds.

If you are going to show your rabbit, then it must be properly prepared for each show. This will mean turning it upside down to groom the underneath and clean the feet, a task that is considerably easier on the Holland Lop than it is for any of the giant breeds.

Large rabbits need large pens; large pens require a lot of bedding and generate a lot of waste that you must dispose of. You must have a regular supply of food, although this is not such a problem these days because most supermarkets sell rabbit food and are open seven days a week.

Whether you want your rabbit as a pet or for showing and breeding purposes, you want a healthy specimen that is not carrying diseases or genetic problems, and the only way to do this is to buy from a reputable source. Many pet stores, both large chains and small independents, sell rabbits. However, not every pet store will have an expert on rabbits and rabbit care on staff, so if you have any doubts about the care or quality of the rabbits for sale look elsewhere. Animal shelters and rescue centers also often have rabbits for sale, so consider checking your local shelter.

Similarly, choose an American Rabbit Breeders Association registered breeder (see the ARBA website for a list of breeders), although there is no guarantee the stock will be healthy.

If you intend to buy from a breeder insist on visiting their rabbitry. The breeder must keep their stock in sanitary conditions, and any

ABOVE AND BELOW **Pet rabbits for sale in a pet store.**

19

breeder that values their stock will take pride in their rabbitry. A filthy, untidy rabbitry indicates poor stockmanship and should be avoided. Similarly, anyone selling rabbits cheaply and who cannot sex them or handle them correctly should be avoided.

A genuine breeder who takes pride in their animals will be easily spotted: they will talk freely and knowledgably, and they will handle their stock in a kind manner that shows respect for the animal. However, there is a lot more to look for, but because rabbits are naturally so appealing it is easy to be taken in by anyone selling a cute-looking young rabbit. Please remember that buying rabbits from anyone who is less than reputable is only perpetuating their trade and buying trouble for the future.

The guidelines that follow are intended to ensure you buy a healthy animal that has a pleasant demeanor – one that will not only give you years of happiness but also lead a happy and healthy life.

Buying from a Breeder

Wherever you buy your rabbit from, you must ensure that it is 100 percent healthy; do not even entertain any rabbit that is showing even the slightest signs of any illness. Mentally prepare yourself a checklist; this is similar to what every judge does with every rabbit he or she picks up on the show bench. You may think when watching experienced judges that they couldn't possibly check all these points in such a short space of time, but they do, albeit very quickly and very skilfully.

Buying from a Breeder

1 Only buy through a reputable breeder. You can find the breeders in your area by contacting the American Rabbit Breeders Association or visiting their website or by visiting local rabbit shows. However, the fact that someone is exhibiting at a show or is a member of the ARBA is not in itself a guarantee that they are reputable.

2 Visit the rabbitry; this is most important, as it is only in the rabbitry that you will see how the rabbits are kept. The rabbitry should be well managed and clean with rabbits kept singly in large, spacious cages. Rabbits are inquisitive, and they should come to the front of the cage when you approach it, not cower in a corner at the back.

3 There should be a quarantine section separate from the main rabbitry. No matter how good a rabbitry is, there should be somewhere to isolate a new rabbit coming in or one showing any signs of illness. If there is no such isolation area, then you must assume that all rabbits are kept together whether healthy or not, and this is not a sign of good management.

4 Does the breeder advertise stud bucks for use to other breeders? If so, then you should clearly see these stud animals kept permanently isolated from the rest of the stock.

5 You should ask to see and if possible handle the parents of the rabbit you are intending to buy. If they are not of a pleasant disposition, then ask yourself what your little bundle of fluff might grow up to be like.

A typical rabbit breeder's "shed."

If you feel confident enough to carry out the physical checks yourself, ask the pet store staff or breeder if they mind you handling the rabbit and checking it over. However, if you do not feel confident enough to do so yourself, you could ask the seller to show you each of the points that follow. If these checks are not carried out with both you and the owner present, then you can only rely on the owner's honesty and will not have any recourse should something turn out to be other than you had been lead to expect. So either you, or the seller with you watching, should carry out a rabbit health check.

Color and Pattern

If you intend to show at ARBA-supported shows or breed from the rabbit, then carefully check that its color and pattern is as it should be. You may have to study the ARBA *Standard of Perfection* because any rabbit that doesn't have the correct color or pattern will never win at ARBA-supported shows, although it may still do well in local pet shows. Color is certainly very difficult to assess in a youngster, and it is probably the one facet of the rabbit that you are going to have to trust the breeder's word on.

Rabbit Health Check

Start at the front of the rabbit and work toward the back end checking all of the following:

Nose should be clear and dry with no discharge.

Teeth should be clean and white. The top teeth should just overlap the bottom ones; do not be fooled if the teeth meet and the breeder tells you that they will come right as they grow older – they won't.

Eyes should be clear and bright with no discharge of any kind. If the third eyelid (in the front corner of the eye) is out it is a sign of stress; ask yourself why the rabbit is stressed – lack of handling usually.

Ears should show no signs of damage; most nicks or cuts in ears do not heal over completely. The ear should be clean and free from any waxing or sign of disease. For any of the lop-eared rabbits, if the ears are not set correctly (i.e. hanging close to the cheeks) there really is no simple answer. If the rabbit has enough width across the skull, then the ears may well descend to the correct position in time, but similarly they may not. Again, a good look at both parents should tell what is likely to happen.

Front and back legs should be straight and strong. Turn the rabbit over on its back and look at the front feet: they should be clean if the babies have been raised in good conditions. The **pads** should be well furred. Check the inside of the front legs for any matting; rabbits use the inside of their front legs to wipe their noses, so any matting may indicate some nasal discharge. Check the **nails**. Look for white toenails – in a colored rabbit this is a fault, and if you intend to show or breed from the rabbit then it must be discounted because it is an inherited trait and will be passed on to its progeny. Has it got all its toes and a **dewclaw** with no deformities? Check the young rabbit's **back legs and feet** while it is lying on its back in your hand – the back legs should lie parallel to the body. Check the toes and toenails as you did for the front feet.

The genitals should be clean and free from any signs of disease. This is probably the first place you will see signs of general ill health.

Sit the rabbit back on its feet.

Run your hands over its back, and with your fingers feel along the ribs and up into the groin. There should be no lumps or irregularities; look especially for a hernia, a small pealike lump in the middle of the stomach. Check the coat for bald patches or any infestation; rabbit fleas are not uncommon and can usually be seen in the very thin fur around the ears or on the belly.

The tail should be straight with no kinks or breaks in it; run your fingers carefully up the tail and check for any irregularities.

A healthy rabbit enjoys a run in the yard.

Ear Numbers

If you intend to show the rabbit at ARBA-sponsored shows, it must have an identification number tattooed on the inside of its left ear. It is the breeder's responsibility to give the rabbit its ear number, and each breeder has their own numbering system. Rabbits cannot be registered with the ARBA until they are at least six months old, so you are likely to register your own rabbit, and the ear number is required for this.

A well-marked Butterfly Holland Lop.

A judge checks a rabbit.

Showing

If you are purchasing the rabbit with a view to showing it, then you should have studied the appropriate section of the ARBA's *Standard of Perfection* before going to see the rabbit. It is also worthwhile to spend some time at a show studying the winners; try to fix the look of the winners in your mind. When you are in the breeder's rabbitry ask if you can "pose" the rabbit (sit it in position as it would be on the show bench), and try to assess its qualities. This is not easy, especially if you have an experienced breeder breathing down your neck, but do not worry because it is exactly what they would do if they were looking at a rabbit with a view to buying it. No breeder is going to sell you their best rabbit, they have bred that for themselves, but you must be ruthless in your decision because soft-heartedness means you may be stuck with a rabbit that never even gets placed. All rabbits go through a gangly stage, which is the period of maximum bone growth, from about six weeks to about 14 weeks, and while they may look like a miniature version of the adult when about four weeks old, the period of bone growth is not yet complete. This must therefore be taken into consideration and makes the selecting of a potential winner all the more difficult.

Age

It is not recommended for a breeder to sell a baby rabbit under the age of eight weeks;

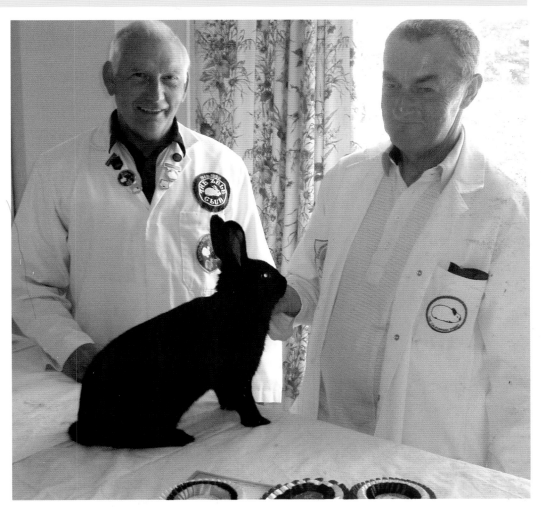

Judge and breeder with the Best in Show – a proud moment.

however, even at eight weeks old the kits are susceptible to stress-related disorders. It is best not to buy a rabbit until it is about 12–14 weeks old, by which time it will be past the danger period for stress-related disorders and should make an illness-free transfer to your rabbitry. Be very wary of stores or breeders that try to sell very young rabbits; they may look cute, but when they are this age they can develop gastric troubles that can be fatal.

Food

The seller (pet store or breeder) should supply you with at least enough food for the rabbit for one week. This will allow you to gradually mix your chosen food in with what the rabbit is used to eating, so that the transition does not bring on stomach upset.

Grooming

If you have not groomed or cut the nails on the breed of rabbit you are buying, get the seller to show you how to do it. There is considerable skill in grooming a long-haired rabbit; if you are not going to have the time or patience to groom on a regular basis, then you should avoid the long-haired breeds. Similarly, turning a full-grown French Lop over to cut its nails is not for the faint hearted. Cutting a rabbit's nails is not difficult and is a skill that every owner must learn.

Temperament

This can be very difficult to assess in a fluffy young rabbit, as almost without exception they are beautiful, loving and cute when young. So what can you do to assess the future temperament of the baby you wish to purchase? First of all, the older the kit is, the more likely it is that any behavior problem will show itself. By the age of about 14 weeks the young rabbit can be compared to a teenager, and it is at this age that undesirable traits are likely to manifest themselves. So if you buy a very young rabbit, between eight and 14 weeks, then you really have no clue to future behavior other than assessing the parent's temperaments and watching the way the seller handles their stock.

Rabbits that have been well handled from a very young age by an experienced breeder will invariably develop into loving, sociable adults.

The process of choosing a young rabbit, whether it is for a pet or for showing, is very important. Of course, most sellers of rabbits are people who love their rabbits and do everything they can to breed and sell healthy specimens; unfortunately, as in most hobbies, there are people out there who are out to con you. You cannot be too careful, as your baby rabbit may well live for up to 10 years, so take your time making your choice. Rabbits are beautiful animals, and the greatest pitfall is that they are exceptionally cute when young, so do not let your heart rule your head. If you want your rabbit as a pet, you simply want a healthy animal; if you want it for showing, you want a healthy rabbit that exhibits the qualities required by the *Standard of Perfection*.

There are many rabbit rescue centers throughout North America. Pictured here is the Greenwich Rabbit Rescue center in London, Enland.

Rabbit Re-Homing and Rescue Centers

Unfortunately, many, far too many, rabbits become unwanted for a variety of reasons and wind up in rabbit rescue centers. Of course, one of the good traits in our society is that there are always caring individuals who will, for no financial reward, look after these abandoned creatures. If you are looking for a rabbit as a pet, then you may be able to find it in your heart to adopt a rabbit from a rescue center. It will be healthy – the rescue centers would not put a sick animal up for re-homing – and it may well already be neutered/castrated. You may be asked to contribute toward the costs of desexing and

houseing the rabbit, but you will be giving a rabbit that did not get the best start in life a second chance and freeing up a space in the rescue center for another unwanted rabbit to be rescued.

There are rescue centers throughout North America, and many have websites. A search engine such as Google will likely yield results, and you can also contact your local animal shelter, which may be able to direct you to a rescue center or have rabbits available for adoption. You may be able to give a rescue rabbit a home.

3 • Feeding Your Rabbit

Rabbits are HERBIVORES; their diet consists almost entirely of vegetable matter. In the wild, herbivores (including rabbits) spend much of their time feeding or grazing, and our domesticated rabbits need the activity of feeding over a long period of each day. To achieve this long eating period we must feed a balanced and varied diet.

The Essential Rabbit Diet

- Concentrated rabbit pellets or a specially prepared rabbit mix
- Fresh, raw fruit or vegetables
- Sweet meadow hay
- Fresh, clean water available at all times

While it is quite possible to make up your own feed for your rabbit using rolled oats, bran, fish meal or soya flour, linseed cake and maize meal, really good commercially produced rabbit feeds are readily available and cheap, so there is really little point. Experts have researched the correct balance of proteins, fats, carbohydrates, vitamins and minerals that a rabbit should have in its diet, and these are combined in commercially available rabbit feeds. Unless you are an animal nutritionist it really is not worthwhile creating your own feeds.

In a good pet store you will find an array of different rabbit feeds, and it will be up to you to decide which one to give to your rabbit. There are basically two types of rabbit feed: "rabbit pellets" and "rabbit mix." Rabbit pellets are just that; they are a uniform brown in color and contain all the required nutrients for the rabbit's diet. A rabbit mix has been made to look attractive, with a variety of grains and vegetables in a variety of colors, usually attractively packaged with pictures of cute little bunnies. In the United States 90 percent of all rabbits are fed on pellets, whereas in the United Kingdom most rabbit breeders and exhibitors feed rabbit pellets, and most British pet-rabbit owners feed mixes. This defines the

A plastic gravity feed bin allows the rabbit to feed on demand and avoids food being left on the pen floor, where it can become contaminated. The bin is easily kept clean.

historic difference between breeders and pet owners in Britain.

Why the difference? It would be easy to say that it is mainly down to marketing: pellets look unattractive and boring, while many of the mixes look and even smell really nice. In reality it really does not matter how the food is presented to the rabbit, so long as it is given all the nutrients it requires and it eats them all. And here lies the problem with mixes, which allow the rabbit to eat selectively, potentially missing vital nutrients, while pellets guarantee the rabbit gets the complete diet it requires.

In fact, it is the breakdown of the content of the food that is far more important than its presentation method. It is normal to feed high-

Rabbit pellets

Rabbit mix

protein (16–18 percent) food to rabbits that have a demanding lifestyle (i.e., show rabbits, breeding does, stud bucks), whereas the more sedentary rabbits (i.e., pets, resting or retired breeding does) are fed on a low-protein (12–14 percent) diet. If your rabbit is a selective eater and leaves certain items in a rabbit mix, then perhaps it would be best to feed it pellets. Otherwise, a commercially marketed rabbit mix with a protein level of between 12 and 14 percent will be quite adequate to form the basis of the diet.

Fruit and Vegetables that Rabbits Particularly Like

- Apples
- Brussels sprouts
- Cabbage
- Carrots
- Cauliflower
- Celery
- Chicory
- Kale
- Lettuce (they like it, but it is not particularly good for them)
- Parsnip
- Pears
- Peas and their pods
- Spinach
- Swede
- Turnip

You can, however, be creative in the fresh fruit and vegetables that you supplement the diet with. Feed only a little each day of what is in season or you have left over. Any fruit or vegetables that you feed your rabbit must be fresh and clean. Stale, rotten or dirty leftover fruit and vegetables are best consigned to the compost heap, not fed to your rabbit, because their stomachs are quite delicate and very easily upset. Never feed greens to rabbits under 12 weeks of age because their stomachs are not developed enough to digest them.

Hay of the very best quality is a vital ingredient of a rabbit's diet; chewing the long strands of hay grinds their teeth, keeping them short and healthy, while the absorption of the roughage is a vital part of the rabbit's digestive system. Added to this is the fact that it takes them a long time to "chew" the hay, which is very similar to their "grazing" in the wild and prevents them from getting bored. Fresh, sweet (yes, it should actually smell quite sweet) hay should be placed in a hayrack securely mounted on the wall of the rabbit's pen so that it can feed whenever it feels like it throughout the waking day.

The fourth and final vital element of the rabbit's diet is fresh water, which should be available at all times, preferably through a drip-feed bottle mounted through the wire mesh on the front of the cage.

Food hygiene is just as important with your rabbit's food as it is with your own food.
- Fresh food must be given every day, and any food left over from the previous day should be removed and disposed of.

A rex rabbit enjoys his hay from a hayrack.

Drinking from a bowl.

- Vegetables and fruits that get dropped on the pen floor will almost certainly become contaminated and will not be eaten by the rabbit; therefore, they should be removed.
- All food bowls should be thoroughly washed on a regular basis.
- Water bottles should be kept scrupulously clean and refilled daily.
- Hay should be provided in a hayrack to prevent it from being trampled into the bedding.

How Much to Feed and When

Rabbits are creatures of habit; consequently, the "when" is just as important as the "how much." You can feed your rabbit once, twice or even three times a day; twice is probably the most popular and most "normal" for the majority of rabbits.

The daily ration of dry pellets or rabbit mix can be split in two, with half given in the morning and the other half at night; similarly split the hay ration into two feeds. Vegetables

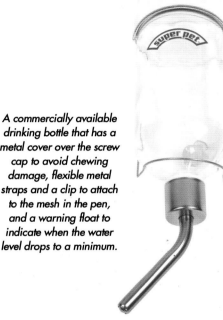

A commercially available drinking bottle that has a metal cover over the screw cap to avoid chewing damage, flexible metal straps and a clip to attach to the mesh in the pen, and a warning float to indicate when the water level drops to a minimum.

TIP Clean the inside of the water bottle

1 Take the top off the bottle and put ½ inch (1.3 cm) of warm water in it.
2 Place a length of chain – sink plug chain is ideal – in the bottle.
3 Place your thumb over top of bottle.
4 Shake vigorously.
5 Empty the water and chain out of bottle.
6 Rinse thoroughly with clean water.
7 Refill and replace top.

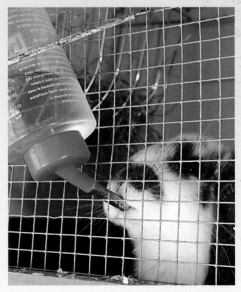

Water bottle clipped to outside of cage.

may be given at lunchtime – to break the day up if you are going to be around every lunchtime – otherwise you may decide to give the vegetables with the morning feed. To keep to a routine of feeding is more important than what you give or when you give it. Work out feeding times to suit your lifestyle and stick to them.

It is quite difficult to work out exactly how much pellet or rabbit mix to give to your rabbit.

You can

1 Stick to the recommended quantities for the breed (e.g. 2 ounces/57g of pellets per day for a Holland Lop). But just like humans, individual rabbits' metabolisms vary: some will be quite active and require a lot of food, whereas a lazy rabbit will not need so much.

TIP Measure the food

Once you have calculated your rabbit's ration per meal, find a suitable container such as a yogurt container, mark a line on it corresponding to the ration per meal, and then just use the container to scoop out the same ration every time.

Daily rations

2 Ask the breeder what they feed their adults and stick to that. Probably quite a sound method, but then do you eat the same as your mother or father?

3 The trial and reduce method. A rabbit should eat its dry ration (pellets or rabbit mix) within an hour of being fed. Using the recommended amount for the breed (per 1 above), watch to see how long it takes your rabbit to empty its bowl. If it does not empty the bowl within the hour then slightly reduce the ration; if the rabbit dives at the bowl and empties it within minutes then add a little until the correct amount is found.

Your rabbit's rations may have to be adjusted throughout the year. In summer you may let it out to roam in the yard where, although it is grazing on your grass (and maybe anything else that is growing), it is getting a lot more exercise and, therefore, may need more feed. In winter although "confined to quarters" for a longer period, it may need more to eat to generate heat to combat the effects of the cold. So yes, be sensible and try and feed the same

TIP Prevent obesity

Decrease food quantity as your rabbit ages. Prevent obesity at all cost; it is as much a killer in rabbits as it is in humans.

TIP Tasty treat

Keep leftover brown bread (white will not do), and when you take your dinner out of the oven put the bread on a rack in the hot, but cooling, oven. It will bake into the tastiest treat that you could possibly give your rabbit. They absolutely love it.

every day, but at the same time be prepared to be flexible.

Treats

The feeding of treats to rabbits over and above the daily ration is a highly contentious subject.

What will you use as a treat? Pet stores have many proprietary brands of rabbit treats, and, of course, just like giving your children candies, there is nothing wrong with these in moderation. But it could just as easily be a tasty leaf picked from the garden or my rabbit's favorite treat – baked dry brown bread.

Wild and Garden Plants

Rabbits will relish many of the wild plants collected from the countryside, such as avens, agrimony, bramble blackberry, burnet, broom, coltsfoot, comfrey, cow parsnip, dock, goose grass, groundsel, heather, hedge parsley, knapweed, nettles, shepherd's purse, sow thistle, trefoil, vetches and yarrow. They also love to

Green leaves are a tasty treat for this lop.

graze on grass and the weeds in it, such as plantains, chickweed, dandelion and clover. There are whole books devoted to the plants that you can and cannot feed to your rabbit, but in the urban society in which we live today can you actually recognize all the wild plants? Once you have recognized them can you guarantee that they are not contaminated with weed killers, fertilizers, car fumes or even other animals (especially dogs and cats) fouling? Unless you are a real country person who knows your plants and is happy that they are unpolluted, then perhaps it is better to make the "green" part of your rabbit's diet up from vegetable leftovers and fruit.

Rabbit Likes

VEGETABLES	FRUIT
Beets	Grapes
Chicory	Apples
Carrots	Pears
Cabbage	Banana
Jerusalem artichokes	Strawberry leaves
Kohlrabi	Raspberry leaves
Kale	
Cauliflower	
Lettuce	
Sunflowers	
Swedes	

Feeding Dos

- Feed at the same time every day
- Remove any uneaten food from the day before
- Wash fruits and vegetables before feeding
- Give raw, fresh vegetables – not cooked or frozen
- A mixture of vegetables is better than a lot of one kind
- Make sure fresh hay is always available, in hayrack
- Fresh, clean water must be available at all times
- Introduce any new kind of food gradually
- Keep all rabbit food in a vermin-proof container

Feeding Don'ts

- Don't make sudden changes to the diet
- Don't feed frosted or stale green food or roots
- Don't gather green food from areas where it could have been fouled
- Don't gather green food from beside busy roads
- Don't leave grass or greens in a heap where they can start to heat up
- Don't feed from the pen floor, where food can become contaminated

The Essentials of Good Rabbit Housing

- Space for the rabbit to live and exercise
- Durability to keep the rabbit comfortable in all weather
- Robust construction to prevent the rabbit from destroying it
- Hygienic conditions
- A secure pen that the rabbit cannot escape, and that predators cannot enter

Never has a popular phrase been more opposite than "buy in haste, regret at your leisure" when talking about the purchasing of rabbit housing. There are so many pens and runs to choose from, and they vary from a penthouse suite to a drafty shack. Buy the biggest and best that you can afford; your initial outlay will be repaid in the long run, and your rabbit will thank you for it.

Space for the Rabbit to Live and Exercise

There is no specific size requirement laid down for a rabbit pen, as each breed varies in shape and size, and more than one may be kept in the same pen.

Wild rabbits spend nearly two-thirds of their day underground in cramped burrows; similarly, our domestic rabbits spend much of their day resting. The size of the pen is not always as important as the size of the exercise area and the amount of time the rabbit has access to it. Bearing this in mind, it is probably best to have a pen with a run permanently attached.

Durability to Survive the Weather

While many North Americans do not suffer the extremes of weather that some others do, any outdoor rabbit pen is going to have to withstand quite a battering in the course of its lifetime, and obviously we would like the pen to have as long a life as possible. A poorly

TIP Size of the Housing

The British *Welfare Livestock Regulations* (1994) provide some interesting and very specific guidelines regarding rabbit housing. These regulations state that housing be "(a) of sufficient size to allow the rabbits to move around and to feed and drink without difficulty and to enable all the rabbits kept in them to lie on their sides at the same time; and (b) of sufficient height to allow the rabbits to sit upright on all four feet without their ears touching the top of the cage." The regulations also state that for "any accommodation that is exposed to the weather, suitable steps shall be taken so as to ensure that the rabbits have access to shelter from the action of the weather (including direct sunlight)."

constructed plywood pen is clearly not going to last long, nor is it probably going to keep the rabbit warm and dry. An outdoor pen should be constructed using heavy-duty tongue-and-groove timber that is either treated with a non-poisonous wood preservative or covered in a waterproof material, such as roofing felt.

Naturally you want your rabbit to have plenty of room and to be comfortable in its pen, but the main function of the pen is to allow the rabbit to escape from the worst of the weather. In the wild, rabbits simply go

A really big traditional pen.

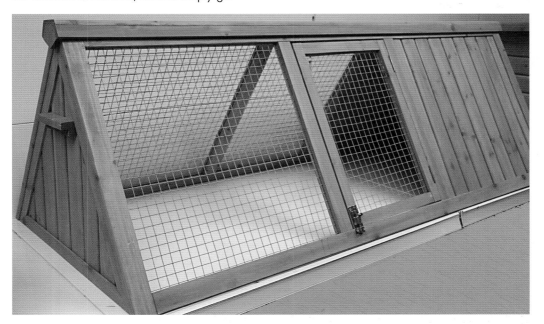

Morant run with shelter at one end.

A delux pen

down into their burrows to avoid weather that does not suit them. Your rabbit's pen should have an area where the rabbit can shelter from the wind and rain; rabbits do not mind mild cold, in fact many thrive in the coldness of a mild winter, but they cannot tolerate dampness. While a good pen will have an enclosed sleeping area where a rabbit can shelter from high or low temperatures, high winds or driving rain, many pens have either shutters (with ventilation holes) or drop-down covers that can be put in place during bad weather.

Robustness to Prevent Damage

Rabbits chew. In the wild they are used to chewing through tree roots that get in their way in the burrow. In a pen they are highly likely to chew any wooden surface they can get their teeth around. The best way to prevent them from damaging their pens is to prevent boredom by providing plenty of distractions; exercise areas with plenty of stimulating things to do and, of course, plenty of companionship – even if it is human companionship it will help reduce the damage. But it is another reason for having a really robust pen that will stand up to what can be pretty hard treatment.

In most pens it is the flooring that will fail first. The wood used to make the floor of the rabbit pen should be at least ¼ inch (6 mm) thick, and it should be treated with an animal-friendly sealant. The edges should be glued as well as nailed to prevent seepage. Regular cleaning of the "dirty corner" or, even better,

training the rabbit to use a litter tray will prevent a lot of urine damage to the floor.

Keep the Rabbit in Hygienic Conditions

Rabbits must be kept in sanitary conditions, and ideally your rabbit's housing should also be visually attractive – who wants an eyesore in their backyard? You can build your own pen if you have good building skills, otherwise you are probably better off going with a store-bought pen.

It is important that the design of the pen is such that it is easy for the owner to reach every corner during cleaning. The wood should be treated in such a way as to prevent urine and feces seeping into it.

Raising the pen at least 1–2 feet (30.5–61 cm) above the ground and keeping it at least 9 inches (25 cm) away from the wall allows air to circulate around the pen, aiding ventilation and the drying of any damp wood. While rabbits don't like damp conditions neither does the wood the pen is built of; damp wood rots and allows pathogens to build up.

Keep the Rabbit Secure

Surely there could be few worse shocks than to go out to your rabbit in the morning and find the pen door open and your rabbit gone! A pen must be secure; it must keep your rabbit enclosed and safe.

All door catches on the pen must be able to be secured so that a rabbit getting hold of the inside

of the door with its teeth and vigorously shaking it does not allow it to fall open. Most pet rabbits will not survive long in the wild, especially in the winter. The rabbit's pen is its home, and it should be sufficiently strong to keep the rabbit enclosed, and safe, while it is unattended.

Keep the Rabbit Safe from Predators

Your rabbit's natural reaction to an attack is fear and flight; in the wild a rabbit races for its burrow at the first sign of attack. In a pen the rabbit literally has nowhere to go should it come under attack from a predator, although it can hide in an enclosed sleeping compartment if it has one. A pen must be strong and secure

LEFT Many dogs will live happily with rabbits – but not all of them.

A super pen with run attached.

43

Checklist for Outdoor Rabbit

- Pen
- Outdoor run – may be attached to pen
- Cover for inclement weather
- Wood shavings
- Barley straw – for bedding
- Ceramic food dishes
- Drip-feed water bottle
- Hayrack
- Sweet meadow hay
- Food
- Toys/chews
- Grooming kit
- Cleaning-out kit – dustpan and brush, scraper, bucket and scrubber

so that an attacking predator could not knock it over. Catches must be secure so that a predator could not open the pen and attack the rabbit. Wire mesh should be no more than 1 x ½ inch (2.5 x 1.5 cm) so that a cat cannot get its paw in through the wire.

Predators can be persistent once they learn where a rabbit lives; even if your pen is secure, a rabbit that is threatened night after night by a hungry predator will suffer from stress and may well even die from the effects of the trauma. If you suspect the presence of a predator the pen and rabbit should be lifted into a shed for a few nights until the predator has lost interest.

Every effort must be made to keep the rabbit pen and surrounding area free from rats and mice; vermin will not only bring disease into your rabbit's pen but also terrify the rabbit.

Positioning your Rabbit Pen

Correctly siting your rabbit's pen is vitally important. The pen needs to be in a sheltered position. It should not face the midday sun or the prevailing wind direction, and it should be close to the house so that all members of the family are encouraged to visit the rabbit and give it the social interaction that it needs.

Healthy rabbits are quite hardy animals and quite tolerant of the cold as long as they are dry. The addition of plenty of clean, dry straw will keep your rabbit quite comfortable on a frosty night. But if the forecast is for wind and rain or snow then the pen may either have to be moved to a more sheltered spot or have a suitably ventilated cover dropped over the front.

Sun and heat are far more dangerous to rabbits than cold weather; in the wild, rabbits retreat to the coolness of their burrows during the heat of the day, but a rabbit "trapped" in a pen exposed to the full sun may well die of heat exhaustion. There are many ways to overcome the ill effects of the sun, but they must be planned before leaving for the day. The pen may have to be moved so it's under trees or in another shaded position, temporary shade can be erected, frozen bottles of water can be put in the pen for the rabbit to lie against, ceramic tiles can be placed in the pen to give the rabbit a cool spot to lie on, or a hose could be laid to run cold water over the top of the pen. There is so much that can be done, but it does require thought before the event — it is too late when the rabbit is lying on its side panting from heat exhaustion.

House Rabbits

Cages and pens for house rabbits are widely available in pet stores; just like outdoor rabbit pens they vary vastly in quality and price. The pet store staff should be able to help you and answer any questions you may have, but you can also consult your local rabbit association for advice.

A small, colorful mobile toy helps to keep the pen-bound rabbit entertained and stimulated.

Rabbits train very easily to use a litter tray.

45

An indoor cage must be carefully sited.

A plastic litter tray is easily kept clean, and odor-absorbing litter granules will help to keep the indoor pen smelling sweet.

Checklist for a House Rabbit

- Purpose-built indoor rabbit cage
- Rabbit play pen
- Litter tray
- Wood shavings
- Drip-feed water bottle
- Ceramic feed bowls
- Hayrack
- Sweet meadow hay
- Food
- Toys/chews
- Grooming kit
- Cleaning-out kit – dustpan and brush, scraper, bucket and scrubber, disinfectant

Siting of a house-rabbit cage is just as important as siting an outdoor pen. It must not be in a draft or beside a heater that will cause the temperature to rise and fall as the heater comes on and goes off, or beside a window that could trap the rabbit in the midday sun. While you will want your house rabbit to be part of the family activities, you do not want the cage in the way where people are constantly tripping over it.

Is your rabbit to live in a house with other pets? If so, then its cage should be somewhere where it can have private time away from the other pets when it needs it.

Is your rabbit to live in a house with children? If so, then it should not have its cage in a child's (or anyone else's) bedroom – rabbits can be active through much of the night and very early in the morning.

Puppy pens and child stair gates can be used to allow your rabbit a safe play/exercise area out of its cage yet in the house.

Hygiene will be a very important consideration in a house rabbit's cage; plastic cages are obviously easy to clean, but always look for a cage with a deep base unit that will contain the shavings that the rabbit will undoubtedly cratch around in. You do not want to be continually vacuuming shavings out of your carpet.

Rabbits can be trained very easily to use a litter tray that can more conveniently be kept clean and hygienic. Use wood shavings in the litter tray, not cat litter, and position it where the rabbit can access it easily.

PART TWO

Keeping Your Rabbit Happy and Healthy

5 • Rabbits: Caring Through the Seasons

Spring

- Check run if it has been stored away since summer. Make any necessary repairs or buy a new one.
- If the weather is dry for a few days let your rabbit out in the run for short periods. Be careful it does not gorge on wet greens and upset its stomach.
- Spring-clean the pen on a sunny, warm, dry day.
- Put the rabbit in the run or somewhere secure for the day.
- Empty the pen of all material.
- Check for any repairs that may need doing – carry out repairs.
- Thoroughly scrub inside the pen using "pet" disinfectant.
- Use a blowtorch to scorch the inside of the pen, paying particular attention to

Pen scraper

cracks and joints. This may be quite a dangerous thing to do, and all relevant safety precautions should be taken. If you are unsure then you should find someone to help you who is proficient at using a lowtorch or paint stripper. The advantage of using this method is that you can get right into the cracks and joints in the pen and destroy any microorganisms that could develop during the heat of the summer.

- Allow to dry completely.
- Replace any damaged or worn equipment – bowl, bottle, hayrack, litter tray, toys or gnawing blocks.
- Replace old bedding and food with fresh stock.
- Place your rabbit back in its pen.
- Check fly screens are in place and ready for the summer.

Assemble your cleaning kit before you start.

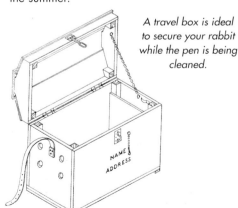

A travel box is ideal to secure your rabbit while the pen is being cleaned.

➤ Put bottles of water in your freezer, ready for hot summer days.

➤ Take your rabbit to the vet for its biannual check.

Summer

➤ Ensure the run and pen are in a position shaded from full sunlight.

➤ Put fly screens/fly protection in place.

➤ Give plenty of exercise – preferably early morning or in the cooler evening.

➤ Be especially vigilant for diarrhea – take immediate action to clean your rabbit to avoid flies (see Fly Strike, pages 75–76).

➤ Do not leave uneaten food in the pen to rot and attract unwanted microorganisms.

➤ Watch the daily weather forecast so that you can be prepared on especially hot days to:

- Move the pen to full shade.
- Run water over the pen.
- Place a wet towel over the door opening.
- Place a frozen brick or bottle of water in the pen for the rabbit to lay against.
- Place a ceramic tile in the pen for the rabbit to lay on.
- Place a bowl of cool, fresh water in the pen.

➤ Do not leave the rabbit unattended for lengthy periods; if you must go away then get a neighbor to check it frequently.

➤ Let the rabbit enjoy a variety of fresh greens that are available at this time of year; it will help build up immunity and strength for the coming winter.

Make sure only fresh greens are left in the rabbit's bowl.

Summer is a good time for a run in the yard.

Pen fans can help keep rabbits cool during hot weather.

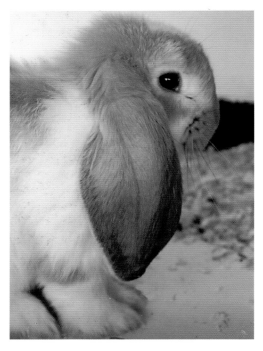

Check the bedding is not damp.

⚔ Fireworks scare rabbits. You may have to make arrangements to bring your rabbit into the house on nights when the fireworks are particularly disruptive.

Autumn

⚔ Move the pen if needed so it will benefit from any winter sun that is available.

⚔ Make sure the new position of the pen is out of the prevailing wind.

⚔ Check waterproofing on the pen.

⚔ Ensure the pen stands about 10 inches (25 cm) away from any wall to allow air circulation.

⚔ Fit storm flap (with ventilation) to the pen.

⚔ Store the run during the winter if the weather will be wet or snowy.

⚔ Cold will probably not be a problem at this time of year, but damp may, so make sure your daily routine includes checking the bedding is dry.

⚔ Where do you store your food, hay and straw? Remember that vermin will be looking for a cozy place to stay for the winter; make sure it will not be in your food or bedding.

Winter

⚔ Make sure you have a clear, dry path to the pen.

⚔ Rabbits can tolerate some cold, but they do not like to be damp, so fit a storm flap when the weather is really bad to prevent rain or snow from getting into the pen.

⚔ If bedding is kept dry it will not freeze – clean "dirty corners" and replace bedding frequently.

⚔ Add extra dry straw on particularly cold nights.

⚔ Do not destroy your rabbit's regular feeding routine with Christmas treats. They do not know that it is Christmas and will not thank you for an upset stomach.

While you clean out its pen your rabbit can relax.

▶ Have a secure box that you can put your rabbit in while you clean its pen. In the summer you may have let it have a run in the yard while you cleaned out, but you may not be able to do the same in the winter, so it is better to box the rabbit while you clean.

▶ During frosty and freezing weather be sure to check the water bottle frequently, especially first thing in the morning, as a rabbit cannot drink from a frozen bottle. You can now buy insulators for rabbit bottles, but an old sock may do the trick. Keep a spare bottle in the house so that you can replace a frozen bottle and allow the rabbit to drink.

53

6 • Glossary of Rabbit-Related Terms

A

AC – any color.

Ad – adult.

Adult Coat – a rabbit's mature coat that is produced for the first time when it is between six and nine months.

Adult Rabbit – a rabbit over five months old is considered an adult for show purposes (note this does not mean for breeding purposes).

Agouti – the coat pattern found in wild rabbits.

Albino – a red-eyed white rabbit that is recessive to color, which will always breed true when mated together but may genetically mask any other color.

All Rounder Judge – a senior judge who is equally qualified in all breeds.

Any Color – any color or pattern that conforms to the color or pattern of recognized breeds.

AOC – any other color.

AOV – any other variety.

Arch

ARBA – American Rabbit Breeders Association, Inc.

Arch – the gentle curvature of the spine, best seen by viewing the animal in side profile.

ASS – adult stock show.

Astringent – a property of some plants useful in treating scours in that it opposes any laxative effect.

AV – any variety.

Blue-eyed white rabbit.

B

Baby Coat – the rabbit's early or first coat, usually up to three to five months of age.

Bagginess – looseness of coat, particularly around the rump of older rabbits.

Banding – the hair shaft having various colors, particularly in agouti-patterned rabbits.

Barred Feet – lighter stripes on colored feet, a common fault on agouti-, chinchilla- and fox-patterned rabbits.

Barrel – long and round in the body.

Barren, Barrenness – the inability for a doe to bear young; infertility.

Base Color – color of the hair shaft closest to the body.

BEW – blue-eyed white.

BIS (BiS) – best in show.

Blaze – the white marking running up the nose and between the ears in the Dutch.

Bloat – a condition where the stomach and intestines fill up with gas; potentially fatal condition that is extremely hard to cure.

Bloom – the vitality and finish of a coat in good condition.

Bold Eye – a prominent, full eye; the sign of a healthy rabbit.

Bowed Legs – usually seen where the front legs are bent like a bow and curved outward in the middle.

BRC – British Rabbit Council.

Breeder – the owner of the doe at the time she gives birth to the rabbit that will be shown in a competition.

Breeder's Class – a class at a show that is confined to exhibitors who actually bred the rabbits being exhibited.

Brindling – colored or white hairs interspersed in the desired color; a common fault in Sooty Fawns.

Broken Coat – where the coat is adversely affected by molt, exposing the undercoat or new coat coming through.

Butterfly French Lop

Broken Pattern – a random mixture of an accepted color on a white base.

Broody Doe – a doe ready for mating.

Buck – a male rabbit.

Butterfly – a very specific pattern that must carry the butterfly nose marking.

Butterfly Nose Marking – the colored butterflylike pattern on the nose of a butterfly rabbit; exhibition butterflies should have no white on the upper lip and no color on the lower lip.

(C

Carriage – the way and style in which a rabbit bears itself, particularly ears in a lop.

Castration – removal of the male organs of reproduction.

Chain – the spots on the sides of an English rabbit running from neck to loin.

Charlie – a term applied to a rabbit that is extremely light in color; usually a butterfly-patterned rabbit that has insufficient body markings, but usually retains its colored ears and a "Charlie Chaplin" moustache instead of the full butterfly nose markings.

Cheeks – rounded area between the eyes and the jaw.

Cheek Spots – a single spot at the side of the eye in English rabbits.

Chest – the front of the rabbit between the forelegs and the chin.

Chinchillation – the elimination of yellow from the coat, as in Chinchillas. Agouti color is the opposite.

Chopped – having the rump cut off abruptly and falling vertically to the tail instead of being rounded; applied to type.

Clean Cut – the line of demarcation between clear markings with no tendency of one color to run into another.

Cheek spots and chain on an English rabbit.

Cobby – a short and stocky body type that is close coupled and very compact.

Condition – the physical state of the rabbit with reference to its health.

Cow Hocks – hocks that are bent inward causing the feet to turn outward.

Crock – a pot or container, ideally ceramic, for holding the rabbit's feed.

Cross-Breeding – the breeding together of two different breeds or colors of rabbit.

Chinchillation

D

Dam – the mother of a litter.

Definition – in chinchilla- and agouti-patterned rabbits, the clear line of demarcation between the pearling and the undercolor.

Density – the number of hairs per square inch on the skin. Essential in all the fur breeds.

Dewclaw – an extra toe on the inside of the front legs.

Dewlap – the pouch of loose skin under the neck, usually seen in mature does.

Dewlap

Doe – female rabbit.

Drags – intrusion of color into white areas of fur.

Proud mom

E

Ear Label – a small sticky label bearing the rabbit's pen number sometimes used at shows.

Ear Lacing – a colored line of fur that outlines the sides and tips of the ear.

Ear Number – a number tattooed on the inside of a rabbit's left ear to identify it. Many breeders tattoo their rabbits themselves, and there are a number of kits available. Breeders create their own numbering systems, but these numbers are required at ARBA shows.

Eye Circle – The contrasting color circle of fur next to the eye.

Eye Stain – circle of color around the eyes of Himalayans; a fault.

F

Fancier – someone who keeps rabbits for showing rather than solely as pets.

Fancy – the community of rabbit fanciers and rabbit shows.

Fancy Section – one of the four divisions used by the BRC; fancy rabbits are purely show rabbits, e.g. Poles, Netherland Dwarfs and Tans.

Feathering – a division of white and color in a pattern that is irregular or lacking in clear definition.

Fine Boned – a term used to describe a rabbit's bone structure; a Pole is said to be fine boned.

Finish – the desired degree of perfection in condition of coat; a finished rabbit.

Firm Condition – the desired condition where the skeleton is well covered with firm flesh.

First Cross (F1) – the immediate offspring of two pure breeds mated together

Fly Back – when the coat is stroked against the lie it "flies back" as opposed to a "roll-

A fine-boned Pole.

back" coat. Fly back is the desired coat in some breeds, e.g. Polish.

Forefeet – front feet.

Foreign Color – any color of fur, nails or eyes differing from that required by the breed standard.

Foster Mother – a doe used in the rearing of another doe's litter.

Frosty Nose – the sprinkling of hair found on the nose of some tan-patterned breeds, especially foxes, which gives a frosted appearance. It is a fault.

Full Coat – adult coat free from molt; a highly desirable condition.

G

Gestation – the period of pregnancy. Usually between 30 and 32 days.

Ghost – a very light chinchilla with wide pearling and little or no undercolor.

Glossy – a bright coat that reflects the light, as opposed to dull and lifeless appearance of the fur.

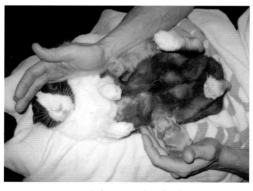

A Dutch foster mother feeding young English Lops.

Groin – the area between the hind legs and the belly.

Guard Hairs – the longer and stronger hairs found in the coat; the presence of guard hairs is particularly important in the roll-back coat.

H

Herringbone – the saddle running down the back of an English resembling the backbone of a herring.

Hock – the last joint on a hind leg.

I

Inbreeding – the mating together of very close relations, such as father and daughter, mother and son, or brother and sister.

Intermediate Coat – the coat prior to the full adult coat that generally appears at about four to five and a half months old.

Iris – the colored portion of the eye, surrounding the pupil.

K

Kindle, In – pregnant doe.

Kindling – the birth of a litter.

L

Lactation – the production of milk by a doe.

Line Breeding – the mating together of rabbits of the same strain, but not so close as that of inbreeding.

Herringbone clearly visible on this Tortoiseshell English.

A newborn litter.

Litter – the youngsters born from a single pregnancy.

Lop Ear – pendulous ears carried below the horizontal, rather than upright.

M

Malocclusion – teeth having the lower incisors extending in front of the upper incisors or meeting with no overlap. This condition may be hereditary, and maloccluded rabbits should not be bred from.

Mandolin – having the appearance of a mandolin laid face down; body arch starting at the back of the shoulders rather than the nape of the neck.

Marked Rabbit – a scab, scar or mark (usually damage, a deformity or mutilation) that identifies a rabbit and is a disqualification at a show.

Mask – the shadings on the face of a rabbit.

Mat – wool or fur tangled in a thick mass, especially in the long-haired breeds.

Mealy Color – a lighter shade of the required color that gives an almost speckled appearance and is undesirable.

Molt – the casting of one coat and the growth of new fur.

Mutation – the sudden origin of an entirely new type, such as the first rex.

Muzzle – the lower part of the face and nose.

Myxomatosis (myxie) – a viral infection spread by mosquitoes, mites and fleas. It is characterized by many skin tumors and is usually fatal. A vaccine has been developed but is not currently available in the U.S.

Judging a class of young English Lops at an agricultural show.

O

Open Coat – a coat that lacks the ability to return to its natural position when stroked toward the head.

Outcrossing – breeding unrelated rabbits or lines within the same breed.

Ovary – the female organ of reproduction.

P

Parasite – another organism that lives on, or within, the host animal. Examples are mange, mites, lice and fleas.

Pearling – the lighter band of color in the chinchilla coat which comes next to the undercoat.

Pea Spots – two spots at the root of the ears when viewed from the front in tan-patterned varieties.

Pedigree – the record of parentage; in rabbits this is not an officially issued document, and anyone can write a pedigree for a rabbit just to record its parentage.

Pendant Ears – hanging ears; essential in lops.

Points – the colored extremities of the rabbit, e.g. in Himalayans.

Pot Belly – enlarged stomach due to fermentation of food causing the formation of gases. Usually due to faulty feeding.

Pseudo Pregnancy (False Pregnancy) – a doe exhibiting all the signs of pregnancy (including nesting) but producing no young.

Points

Putty Nose – white spot on the nose extremity.

R

Racy – a derogatory term meaning long in the body and lacking breadth, especially in the shoulders.

Rat Faced – narrow skull and head.

REW – red-eyed white.

Roll-Back Coat – a gradual return to the normal position of the fur when stroked from the rump to the shoulders; the kind of coat desired in many breeds.

Roman Nose – a nose whose bridge is so comparatively high as to form a slightly convex line from the forehead to the nose tip. An especially pronounced feature in the English Lop.

Rump – the hindquarters of the rabbit.

Run (1) – the intrusion of white color into a color-marked area on a marked breed.

Run (2) – an exercise area, usually made from wire netting, for the rabbit; the run may

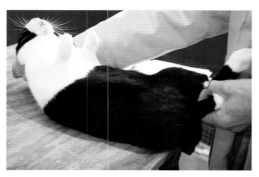

A judge checks a rabbit.

be either attached permanently to the rabbit's pen or detached.

Rusty Color – as applied to black or blue rabbits, a rusty tinge that can be caused by exposure to sunlight, crossbreeding or certain stages of the molt. Undesirable.

S

Saddle – the whole upper portion of the back.

Scours – diarrhea

Screw Tail – tail twisted to one side, particularly a problem in the long-tailed breeds, e.g. hares.

This pen has an exercise run downstairs.

Scut – a tail.

Self – the rabbit being the same color all over. Undercolor is usually paler. Examples are REW, BEW, black, blue, brown (chocolate) and lilac.

Shaded Pattern – the pattern found in siamese sables, siamese smokes, seal points and sooty fawns.

Shading – variation in shades from darker on the saddle to lighter on the sides, especially in sables and smokes.

The shaded pattern of a Smoke Pearl Netherland Dwarf.

Shape – the general conformation of a rabbit's overall appearance, as shown by body structure; synonym for type.

Sheen – lustrous effect; brilliance of coat when in peak condition.

Shoulder – that portion of the body from the neck back through the fifth rib and the upper joint of the foreleg.

Silvering – the mixture in the coat of white-tipped guard hairs; desired in Silvers and Meissener Lops, but even a little silvering is a fault in non-silvered breeds.

Sire – father.

Slate – the bottom color in agouti and chinchilla, black, blue and brown.

Smellers – whiskers.

Smut – darker nose markings.

Snipey – narrow, elongated head.

Sore Hock – ulceration above the footpad. Caused on the back hocks by thin bedding or stamping.

Speck Eye – small white specks in the iris of the eye.

The silver coat of a silver gray.

Sperm – the reproductive cells produced by the buck.

Standard – the ARBA publishes its *Standard of Perfection* periodically, outlining the various attributes required of every breed it recognizes. At shows judges evaluate rabbits based on how closely they meet the breed's standards.

Stockings – the dark markings on the legs of Himalayans.

Stops – white markings on the hind feet of Dutch rabbits that cut cleanly into the leg color.

Strain – a genetically related bloodline possessing distinguishing characteristics such as type, color or coat, and the ability to pass the characteristic on to the offspring.

Stud – a collection of rabbits where breeding usually takes place.

Stud Buck – a buck used for mating, and usually no longer used for showing.

T

Tan Pattern – the pattern found in tans, foxes and martens.

Tear Drops – a fault found in English; small colored spots below the eye.

Texture – the quality of the fur; generally, the silkier the coat the better in the fur and rex varieties.

Ticking – hairs of a different color to the main coat; can be desirable in tan-patterned rabbits or unwanted in selfs.

Tipping – the guard hairs.

Tortoiseshell – an alternative term for the color madagascar or sooty fawn. A sandy yellow color with black shadings.

Triangle – a small area behind the ears, which is generally lighter in color than the rest of the coat. A feature of tan- and agouti-patterned rabbits.

Trimming – the illegal removal of hairs to improve the look of an exhibition rabbit.

Tufts – the ear furnishings of an Angora.

Type – the appearance and conformation of the rabbit.

U

Undercolor – the color at the base of the fur shaft or next to the skin.

Undercut – the line of demarcation on the belly between the white saddle and the hindquarters of the Dutch.

Ticking is desirable in this Chocolate Silver Fox.

V

Variety – a distinct breed such as Havana, Angora, Holland Lop as opposed to various colors within a breed.

Vent Disease – a venereal disease in rabbits that affects both sexes and is highly contagious.

VHD – Viral hemorrhagic disease. Fatal in rabbits.

The Swiss Fox is one breed that must not have a woolly coat.

W

Wall-eye – an eye that is whitish on the surface (cornea) with a milky film over the eye. Often appears in one eye only, thus giving the rabbit the appearance of having different colored eyes. A serious fault in show rabbits.

Weaning – the removal of youngsters from their dam.

White Toenail – a nail without pigmentation, showing only pink cast in the blood vessel.

Woolliness – a type of fur showing the character of wool rather than fur; a fault in the Cashmere and Swiss Fox coats.

Wry Neck – carriage of the head to one side at an angular plane, instead of the normal carriage in the vertical plane, often caused by a deep-seated middle ear infection.

7 • Health, Hygiene and Common Rabbit Diseases

Rabbits are naturally healthy animals; a well-fed, well-housed and well-loved rabbit will generally speaking be a happy and vigorous companion. The observant rabbit keeper will spot the slightest downturn in a rabbit's demeanor and quickly take action to prevent the situation from escalating.

10 Big Questions to Ask Yourself Every Time You Feed Your Rabbit

Daily Health Check

1 Is the pen secure? No signs of attempted break-in?
2 Is bedding dry? A damp rabbit is not a happy one.
3 Does your rabbit come forward to greet you? If not, why not?
4 Has your rabbit eaten all of its previous meal – if not, why not?
5 Has water been drunk from the bottle? Check bottle is working first.
6 Is the water bottle completely empty? Check it is not broken.
7 Check droppings in the pen. Is there any sign or smell of diarrhea?
8 Check your rabbit's eyes. Are they bright and alert?
9 Check the rabbit's mouth. Is it clean and dry with no slobbers or dribbles?
10 Check the inside of the rabbit's front legs. No matting or signs of nasal discharge?

Check your rabbit's eyes – are they bright and alert?

Rabbits thrive on routine in their lives; they should be fed at the same time every day, and the main parts of their meals – pellets/mix, hay and water – should be the same every day and delivered in the same way. If you keep to rigid routines with your rabbit you will quickly notice if anything is wrong. If there is no routine it is

Pride in your rabbit.

Children love to be with their rabbits but remember to wash after contact with a rabbit.

Hygiene Rules

1 Wash your hands after handling a rabbit or cleaning out a pen.
2 Wash the rabbit's food bowls and water bottles separately from the household's dishes. Keep a separate bowl for washing the rabbit's bowl and bottle. Do not drain washed rabbit bowls and bottles on the kitchen drainer. Dry the rabbit's bowl and bottle with a towel kept especially for it or with paper towels.
3 Store rabbit food separately from your own, and keep it in sealable containers to prevent access by vermin. Buy dry food in small quantities only so it is fresh when fed to your rabbit.
4 Never bring rabbits into or near the place where your food is stored or prepared.
5 Never eat, drink or smoke while playing with your rabbit or while cleaning out the pen. Be careful to avoid doing anything that may transfer dirt from the rabbit or pen to your lips.
6 When young children play with a rabbit or clean a pen an adult should supervise to ensure that children follow these rules and learn the elements of good hygiene.

hard to spot anything out of the ordinary. Carry out the Daily Health Check (see box, page 70) every time you feed your rabbit.

If you keep more than one rabbit you should have somewhere prepared so you can immediately isolate any rabbit that you suspect is sick. This should be a warm, well-ventilated location away from harsh lighting. Many of the common rabbit ailments are highly contagious; rapid isolation can prevent a disease from spreading to other animals. Many of the rabbit diseases can prove fatal if not treated promptly; the severity of the signs should dictate your next course of action. If the signs are minor, or rather vague, you might wait 12–24 hours to see if things return to normal. If they do not you should contact a veterinarian as soon as possible, as they are the trained experts in small animal care. Do not leave it until later, by which time a simple problem may have escalated into a far more serious one. Rabbits are not good patients; rather than fight an illness, many seem to give up as soon as they feel ill. Quick action is called for.

Some rabbit diseases can be transmitted to humans (they are noted in the list that follows), particularly children. The hygiene rules on the facing page should prevent this from happening.

Clean, secure pens mean happy, healthy rabbits.

Diseases

Abscesses (see also Tapeworm Cyst) – can occur anywhere as a result of cuts or wounds. Should heal if treated promptly by a veterinarian.

Anemia/Listlessness – anemia is easily detected in albino breeds since the red of the eye turns dull or even pink. Give plenty of green foods, especially those rich in iron, e.g. parsley.

Bald Patches – rabbits are born bald and do not start to fur up until about 10 days old. (See also Mange and Ring Worm)

Blindness – rabbits are born blind; their eyes open after about 10 days.

Bloat (Blows) – common condition in half-grown youngsters; the stomach becomes distended and full of gas. Very distressing for the rabbit. The rabbit may be saved by prompt action; seek veterinary advice immediately.

Canker – caused by very small mites that get into the inner surface of the ear and irritate it; there will be a thin discharge from the ear that hardens and forms a crust. The rabbit will shake its head and scratch its ear. The infected ear has a distinctive smell. Can be treated with eardrops from a veterinarian.

Cannibalism – does sometimes eat their young at birth. Thought to be due to thirst; give the doe a large bowl of fresh water at time of kindling.

Coccidiosis – young rabbits will fail to gain weight, sit hunched up in the corner with their back legs extended forward; in bad cases there is severe diarrhea with rapid weight loss and the rabbit has a pot-bellied look. Microscopic parasites infest either the liver or the lining of the intestine. Caused by poor husbandry: young rabbits eating fouled food or drinking water infected with the oocysts or eggs. Some rabbit feeds now have an additive that prevents coccidiosis. Seek veterinary advice immediately.

Conjunctivitis – inflammation of the eye; common in bucks, especially during heavy molt. Eyedrops from a veterinarian should clear the problem.

Constipation – the passing of only a few very dried-up pellets. Increase green foods to cure.

Convulsions – caused by over-mating of either buck or doe, overcrowded conditions as youngsters grow and generally poor, unhealthy conditions in the rabbitry. Isolate any rabbits suffering and radically improve the living conditions in which they are kept; survival a possibility, but future uses for breeding unlikely.

Coprophagy (Re-ingestion) – your rabbit eating its own droppings. This is quite natural. Rabbits have to eat their food twice, and your rabbit is re-ingesting half-eaten food. The half-digested pellet is black, sticky and smelly. If you find a lot of these pellets uneaten in the pen something is disturbing the rabbit from its natural task – is there a dog or cat threatening your rabbit?

Cuts and Wounds – add a drop of mild disinfectant to some boiled and cooled water and bathe the wound gently. If it does not heal within a couple of days seek veterinary advice.

Cyst – there are two types of worm cysts in rabbits. One is found in the liver and the other under the skin. They are caused by rabbits eating green food that has been fouled by dogs. The liver cyst often proves fatal; the ones under the skin do little damage and can be removed by a veterinarian.

Dandruff – usually appears as fine grayish-white scales on the skin and fur behind the neck, where the rabbit may scratch it. Usually appears on rabbits kept in small pens in hot weather. Improving living conditions, exercise and diet will cure it.

Diarrhea (Scours) – may be the symptom of something more serious. Discontinue green food and give hay only. Astringents such as shepherd's purse, strawberry leaves or raspberry leaves will help. If not cured in 24 hours seek veterinary advice.

Ear Canker – see Canker.

Ear Mites – see Canker.

Electric Shock – if your rabbit has bitten through an electric cable and is laying either unconscious or semiconscious, turn off the power before touching the rabbit then cover it with a blanket and keep it warm while you call a veterinarian.

Eyes – if eyes become damaged or eyelids torn, consult a veterinarian. Eyes may become inflamed for a number of reasons: drafts, dust, bucks spraying urine, fumes from urine in the pen. A veterinarian will prescribe eyedrops.

Fleas – like all animals with fur coats, rabbits can get fleas; they are usually seen first where the fur is thinnest, around the ears or on the belly. Black specks of flea droppings will probably be seen before the actual fleas. The rabbit flea is one of the vectors that carry myxomatosis. Flea treatment from a veterinarian will get rid of them.

Fly Strike – fly strike is perhaps the most disgusting thing you will ever see, and it is entirely preventable with good animal husbandry. A fly attracted by the smell of diarrhea lays its eggs in the feces-soiled fur. Within 24 hours the maggots hatch and burrow into the rabbit's flesh, where they eat the rabbit's soft tissue. By the time you discover it, the flesh will be heaving with maggots; the agony this causes the rabbit cannot be imagined. Rabbits discovered to have fly strike should be taken to the vet immediately and possibly put down.

Heat Stroke/Exhaustion – in very hot weather, rabbits enclosed in a pen are liable to get heat stroke. Signs are panting, gasping for air, listlessness and laying on the back to cool the stomach. Prevention is better than cure. Move the pen to a cooler spot; run water over the pen; hang a wet towel over the door area (will need frequent replacing as it dries); place frozen bottles of water in the pen; put a ceramic tile in the pen so the rabbit has something cool to lay on. The cure is to move the rabbit to a cool place, lay a wet towel over it or mist it with cool water, and give it a bowl of cool water. The stress of rushing it to the vet may do more harm than good, unless first-aid treatments are having no effect.

Hernia – a rupture or protrusion of the abdomen contents outside the abdomen. Seek veterinary advice.

Ingrown Eyelash – can be very painful for the rabbit, seek veterinary advice.

Lice – unlike fleas, lice lay their eggs, known as nits, in the fur of the host animal. The eggs are white and attach themselves to the hair shaft. They show up well on dark colored rabbits and can be seen as white specks in the coat when grooming. Seek veterinary advice for treatment. Can be transmitted to humans.

Listeriosis – disease, resembling influenza, caused by an infection with a bactera (listeria) from contaminated food; may cause miscarriages in does. Contagious to humans.

Mange – a parasitic complaint that is caused by small mites burrowing under the skin resulting in scabs that appear first on the head and then on the legs, feet and body. The fur drops out, and the rabbit scratches continually. Seek veterinary advice. Contagious to humans.

Megrims, Dizziness, Fits – nervous disorder; the rabbit may carry its head on one side or swing it from side to side. Usually attributed to a defect in the digestive organs, which affect the nerves. In extreme cases the rabbit has a fit. Careful attention to diet and the addition of dandelion and clover may help. Otherwise seek veterinary advice.

Mites – several different mites affect rabbits. The ear mite causes ear canker, while the forage or harvest mite burrows into the skin and causes intense irritation that the rabbit will scratch until it is raw; this condition is also known as mange (see above).

Mucoid Enteritis – also known as bloat, scours or diarrhea. This infection accounts for a very high percentage of deaths in young rabbits, although it can affect rabbits of all ages. Rabbits appear listless, lose their appetite, have dull, squinting eyes, grit and grind their teeth, are thirsty and stomach contents slosh. The youngster may be constipated or may have diarrhea and pass a clear jellylike substance. Seek veterinary advice; prognosis is not good.

Myxomatosis – deadly viral disease; transmitted from the wild rabbit population by the rabbit flea or mosquitoes. Clinical signs include swelling of the eyelids until the rabbit is unable to open its eyes and swelling of the nose, mouth and anus. Infected rabbits rarely recover.

Paralysis – usually attacks the hindquarters; caused by being dropped, mishandled or attacked by rats, dogs, foxes. Keep warm and quiet for up to two weeks; may recover. Seek veterinary advice.

Pneumonia – acute disease; rabbit holds its head high and tilted backward, breathes with difficulty and has a mucus discharge from mouth, nasal passages and eyes. Prompt veterinary attention may save the rabbit. Usually caused by poor animal husbandry. Seek veterinary advice.

Pseudo-tuberculosis – infected rabbits rapidly lose weight and develop diarrhea. The infection is caught by eating greens soiled by wild birds and other rabbits. It spreads to humans when hands become contaminated with diarrhea and hygiene is inadequate. Seek veterinary advice.

Obesity – Too much food and too little exercise will kill a rabbit. More exercise and less food may save a severely overweight rabbit, but heart failure is highly likely.

Ophthalmia – swollen or closed eyes. Common, especially in young rabbits kept in poor conditions. Improve living conditions, especially ventilation. Bathe eyes with warm saline solution; if no improvement, seek veterinary advice.

Overgrown Claws – clipping rabbit claws is not difficult, and as it is required frequently for pen-kept rabbits it is best to get an experienced rabbit keeper or veterinarian to teach you how to do it (see pages 80–81).

Overgrown Teeth – overgrown teeth are usually a result of bad breeding. A vet can trim the teeth before they get long enough to cause the rabbit discomfort (probably as often as once a month). Check teeth when buying your rabbit and do not buy one with maloccluded teeth (see pages 82–83).

Pot Belly – common condition in half-grown youngsters; the stomach becomes distended and full of gas. Very distressing for the rabbit. The rabbit may be saved by prompt action; seek veterinary advice immediately.

Red Water – Colored urine due to cold and damp affecting kidneys. Too many diuretic greens, e.g. dandelions, may cause the same symptoms, as will too many beets. Ensure the rabbit has warm, dry bedding, and reduce or withhold green food for a couple of days. If no better, seek veterinary advice.

Healthy mother and son enjoy a treat.

Rickets – very weak in legs; common in badly kept rabbitries lacking light and sunshine and wth a diet deficient in vitamins A and D. Improve husbandry and seek veterinary advice.

Ring Worm – a fungal disease that causes circular bald patches on the head and feet. It is especially infectious to children who cuddle their pet rabbit. Seek veterinary advice. Contagious to humans.

Salmonellosis – bacteria associated with food poisoning in humans. Infected rabbits will have diarrhea, and pregnant does may abort litters. Seek veterinary advice. Contagious to humans.

Sexual Inflammation – see Vent Disease.

Slobbers/Acute Indigestion – usually caused by infected teeth or abscesses. The rabbit drools and wipes its mouth with its front legs. Difficult to cure. Seek veterinary advice.

Snuffles (Sneezing) and Colds – infection of the respiratory tract correctly known as contagious rhinitis; characterized by a thick, yellowish discharge from the nose and continual sneezing, and the inside of the rabbit's front legs will become matted where it has wiped its nose with its legs. May develop into pneumonia if not treated quickly; isolate immediately; highly contagious; very difficult to cure. Seek veterinary advice.

Sore Hocks – thin fur on hocks may be an inherited defect. Nervous or stressed rabbits that do a lot of stamping are prone to it, especially if bedding is thin. Seek veterinary advice.

Stoppage of the Bowels – see Constipation.

Swollen Teats/Mastitis – congestion of the milk glands; may occur when a doe loses her litter or has a litter of only one. Mammary glands become hot, hard and painful. Bathing with a warm cloth may help. Otherwise seek veterinary advice.

Tapeworm Cyst – a lump that can appear anywhere on the body and may grow as large as an egg. Usually caused by the rabbit eating green food that has been fouled by a dog. Seek veterinary advice; expect full recovery.

Tick – a parasite that attaches itself to a rabbit and feeds on the rabbit's blood for several days, until sufficiently bloated to drop off naturally. Note: it can only be picked up by the rabbit running free in the yard or by contact with contaminated hay or straw. If this is the case change your supplier.

Tuberculosis – airborne virus; check ventilation in rabbitry. Breathing sounds harsh; rabbit may eat ravenously but lose weight. Isolate immediately. Seek veterinary advice.

Vent Disease – rabbit syphilis; scabs or sores on reproductive organs. If rabbit licks infected reproductive organs scabs will appear on face as well. Highly contagious at mating. Seek veterinary advice.

VHD – viral hemorrhagic disease; fatal.

Worms – small, round worms are very occasionally found in the droppings. Seek veterinary advice.

Wry Neck – rabbit will hold its head to one side and may lose balance; caused by deep-seated ear infection. Seek veterinary advice.

Cutting Rabbit Nails

Just like our nails, rabbits' nails grow continually, and just as we do not wear our toenails down naturally, neither does a rabbit that is kept on soft bedding in a pen. A pen-kept rabbit will need its nails cut at least twice a year, as overgrown nails start by becoming uncomfortable but soon become painful. A rabbit that regularly runs free in the house or yard may need them cut less frequently. Make a nail check part of your weekly health check (see pages 88–90).

If you are unsure of how to hold the rabbit and how to cut the nails, it is best to get either an experienced rabbit keeper or a veterinarian to teach you. The cutting of very large rabbits' nails is not for the fainthearted, as they may struggle and kick out; it is easier if two people work together to cut a large and uncooperative rabbit's nails.

When to Cut the Nails

The cut nail should be about ¼ inch (6 mm) longer than the quick, which can clearly be seen through light colored nails but is more diffficult to see on rabbits with dark nails. When nails are ½–¾ inch (12 mm–19 mm) long they should be cut. Do not forget the dewclaw on the inside of the front legs.

How to Cut Nails

In good natural daylight sit on a low chair or stool so that the top of your legs form a flat base to lay the rabbit on. Lay the rabbit on its back between your legs with its head farthest away from you,

Extra care is required when cutting black nails.

and get it settled and calm. Rabbits will soon settle in this position if they feel secure.

Hold the nail clippers in one hand, your cutting hand, and one of the rabbit's feet in the other. Use your forefinger and thumb to hold the toe of the nail you wish to cut. Cut with your nail clippers fore and aft, not sideways across the nail; make the cut about ¼ inch (6 mm) above the quick. Do all the nails on one foot before moving on to the next foot so that no nails get missed.

Holding your rabbit confidently makes the job so much easier.

TIP The best nail clippers to use

Pet stores sell small dog nail clippers that are ideal for rabbits' nails.

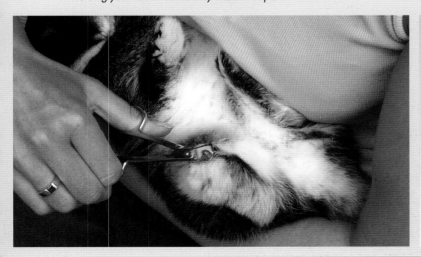

TIP First aid

Pet stores and vets sell a powder that can be applied to stop bleeding should you accidentally cut the quick. It is always worth having such a product handy before you start trimming your rabbit's nails.

Rabbit Teeth

The front, or incisor, teeth of rabbits grow continually throughout their lives. Wild rabbits keep them short by continually gnawing at branches, bark, roots and other hard foods. If you feed your rabbit a proprietary brand of rabbit food (mix or pellets) it should have sufficient hard material in it to wear the rabbit's teeth as it grinds the food down. If your rabbit lacks sufficient gnawing material, its incisor teeth may grow longer and longer until in some cases the rabbit cannot eat. In this case your rabbit should be encouraged to chew by giving it plenty of fresh hay or chewing material, such as cabbage, cauliflower or brussels sprout stalks, or a gnawing block. Pet stores sell a whole range of gnawing products for rabbits.

In some rabbits, the teeth are positioned incorrectly in the mouth so they do not work against each other and wear down properly. This is an inherited trait known as malocclusion. Rabbits suffering from malocclusion should not be used in a breeding program and cannot be shown in rabbit shows. Maloccluded rabbits will need to have their teeth clipped by a veterinarian on a regular basis.

Incorrectly aligned teeth can cause problems.

Class I Malocclusion – the bite is okay (the top teeth line up with the bottom teeth), but the teeth are crooked, crowded or turned.

Class II Malocclusion – the upper teeth stick out past the lower; this is called an overbite or

buck teeth. Rabbits should have a slight overbite but not an excessive one.

Class III Malocclusion – the lower teeth stick out past the upper teeth; this is also called an underbite.

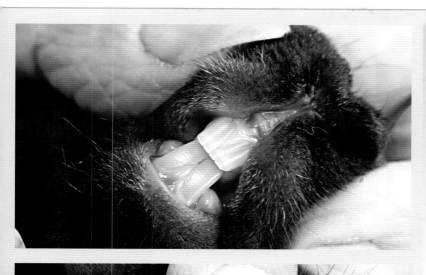

TIP Make your own gnawing block

You can make your own gnawing block from a freshly cut branch – apple is their favorite. Leave the bark on – they love tearing it off and chewing it.

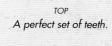

TOP
A perfect set of teeth.

LEFT
Maloccluded teeth.

8 • Rabbit Routines

Animal husbandry or, to be more specific, rabbit husbandry is all about setting up regular routines and sticking to them. In the wild a rabbit's routines are laid down annually, seasonally and even daily, usually being dictated by the weather. Anything that upsets those routines is likely to bring chaos to the rabbit's life – those who have read Richard Adams's wonderful book *Watership Down* will appreciate just how the lives of the main characters were turned upside down by man.

Most of us lead a fairly orderly life, and it really should not be too difficult to fit your rabbit's routines into your everyday lifestyle. Try to establish the following routines for your rabbit:

1. Daily life-pattern routine
2. Daily feeding routine
3. Daily health check
4. Daily cleaning routine
5. Weekly cleaning routine
6. Weekly health check
7. Weekly grooming routine
8. Biannual cleaning routine
9. Biannual health check
10. Seasonal life-pattern routine

1. Daily Life-Pattern Routine

Pen rabbits like to sleep during the hours of darkness in the summer. They also like to sleep during the afternoon in both the summer and winter.

Your rabbit relies on you to set up routines for feeding and cleaning.

➤ Open up and say good morning to your rabbit fairly early in the morning and carry out your
  • Daily health check,
  • Feeding and watering,
  • Daily cleaning.

➤ Play time/human contact time or put it out in the run in the cool of the morning.

➤ Afternoon in pen left in peace to sleep.
  • Early evening contact/training/grooming time followed by the evening feed.

➤ Close up and say good night. Have a final security check either at last light or just before you go to bed.

2. Daily Feeding Routine

Morning
- Clean out any leftover food, greens or hay trodden into the floor.
- Check and replenish hay.
- Wash and refill water bottle.
- Give half of the daily ration of pellets or rabbit mix.
- Give mix of fresh greens.

Evening
- Check water bottle and refill if necessary.
- Give the other half of the daily ration of pellets or rabbit mix.

3. Daily Health Check

Your daily health check will become, with practice, a very quick check over your rabbit to make sure all is well; it should include the checks outlined below.

Does your rabbit come to greet you at the front of the pen? If not, why not?

Has last night's food been eaten? If not, why not?

Has some water been drunk? If not, why not? Check bottle is working properly.

Look into your rabbit's eyes; they should be clear and bright.

Your rabbit should be bright eyed.

Look at your rabbit's nose; it should be clear and dry.

Look at your rabbit's mouth; it should be clear and dry.

Run your hand over your rabbit's back as if stroking it; check for lumps, cuts or scratches.

Human contact time.

Check with your hand, nose and eyes around the back end of your rabbit. Take immediate action if the coat is soiled with diarrhea.

4. Daily Cleaning Routine

Clean food bowl.

Clean water bottle.

Clean out any leftover food or hay that has fallen to the floor.

Clean out the "dirty corner" or litter tray if you have managed to litter train.

Your rabbit's nose should be dry and clean.

A rabbit eating its daily ration.

5. Weekly Cleaning Routine

All rabbit pens should be cleaned out completely at least once a week; in hot weather or for a particularly dirty rabbit it should be done more often.

➤ Move rabbit to a safe location; either place it in a run or "box" it.

➤ Remove all food bowls, toys and gnawing blocks.

➤ Using a dustpan and brush kept especially for the job, clear out all the straw and shavings from the pen. This fouled bedding does make excellent compost for the garden if you have the space to create a compost heap, though it does take a rather long time to rot down (about a year).

➤ Scrub out the inside of the pen using a pet disinfectant; rinse well with clean water.

➤ Allow to dry.

➤ Put a good, deep layer (about 1 inch/25 mm deep) of pet wood shavings on the entire floor of the pen and sleeping compartment.
  • **Do not** put a layer of newspaper under the shavings; rabbits chew the newspaper, and it can form a ball in the gut. As it is indigestible it may block the stomach, with serious consequences.
  • **Do not** use sawdust as a replacement for wood shavings; the dust gets in

the rabbit's eyes, and then it will be a trip to the veterinarian to cure its irritated eyes.

➤ Add a layer of soft, clean barley straw; extra straw in the depths of winter will keep your rabbit warm.

➤ Return clean bowls, bottle, chews and toys to the pen.

➤ Return the rabbit to the pen.

6. Weekly Health Check

Every week when you carry out your weekly cleaning you should carry out a weekly health check on your rabbit. This includes your daily health check but is a lot more thorough and should identify a problem before it gets serious and causes the rabbit discomfort. At first sight it may seem that you have a lot to do, but with a little practice you will find that it actually only takes a couple of minutes, and it will be a couple of minutes well spent.

Start at the front of the rabbit and work toward the back end, checking all of the following:

➤ Nose should be clear and dry with no discharge.

➤ Teeth should be clean and white; the top teeth should barely overlap the bottom ones. Make a check to ensure they have not been damaged and don't have anything stuck in them.

- Eyes should be clear and bright with no discharge of any kind.

- Run your fingers over both ears and check for damage; especially look for nicks or cuts and clean and treat if necessary. Look

in and smell the inside of the ears; they should be clean and free from any waxing or sign of disease.

Turn the rabbit over on its back.

- Look at the front feet; they should be clean. Run your fingers along the legs and feet, checking for any damage. Check the pads

Add a layer of soft barley straw to the clean pen as it provides both warmth and food for your rabbit.

of each foot; they should be well furred. Check the inside of the front legs for any matting; rabbits use the inside of their front legs to wipe their noses, so any matting may indicate some nasal discharge.

➤ Check the nails. If they need cutting, do them now; do not put it off.

➤ Genitals should be clean and free from any signs of disease. This is probably the first place you will see signs of general ill health.

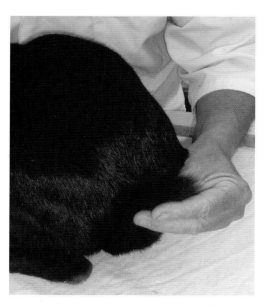

Run your fingers up the length of the tail and check for irregularities.

Sit the rabbit back on its feet.

➤ Run your hands over its back. With your fingers feel along the ribs and up into the groin; there should be no lumps or irregularities. Check the coat for bald patches or any infestation; rabbit fleas are not uncommon and can usually be seen in the very thin fur around the ears or on the belly.

➤ Run your fingers up the length of the tail and check for any irregularities; it should be straight with no kinks or breaks in it.

7. Weekly Grooming Routine

The amount of grooming that is required each week will vary throughout the year, as much more work will be required when your rabbit is molting than during the rest of the year. You can carry out your weekly grooming at the same time as your other weekly tasks (weekly health check and weekly cleaning).

➤ Normal Coat (when your rabbit is not molting):
  • Sit your rabbit on a nonslip grooming table – this can be a small piece of carpet (carpet samples are ideal and free from a carpet store) placed on a table or bench at a suitable height for you to work at.
  • Dampen your hands (rub them with a damp cloth) and then work them from the back end of the rabbit toward its

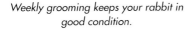

Weekly grooming keeps your rabbit in good condition.

head so that you make the rabbit's coat stand up on end. It will soon return to its normal position. Do this a few times – it will bring out the dead hairs and any dust that the coat has picked up from the wood shavings and straw. You can use a soft dog-grooming brush over the coat, but your dampened hands will do a much better job.

- Use a fine comb (dog grooming ones are best) to very gently comb around the rump of the rabbit. Check the underneath, around the genitals; this area may need combing – do so with *extreme care*.
- Sit the rabbit back on all fours and use a piece of velvet or soft chamois to rub the coat over, working from head to tail this time, and bring out that lovely, healthy shine.

Coat in Molt

- The molt is a natural phenomenon whereby the rabbit replaces its thick winter coat with a new thinner summer coat. It normally takes place during the summer months, but rabbits kept sheltered from the elements can molt at almost any time. It is quite amazing how much hair comes out of a rabbit during its molt, which may last for many weeks.

- You can assist your rabbit through the molt by regular grooming.
- Pet stores sell rubber brushes for grooming cats and dogs; the dog version is a bit hard and heavy for rabbits, but the cat version is absolutely perfect for shifting a molty coat. Use the rubber brush by brushing in the direction of the coat, i.e. from head to tail.
- You can further aid the molt by careful use of a comb – be very careful with the comb, as a rabbit's skin is quite thin and tears very easily.

8. Biannual Cleaning Routine

The big biannual clean is a complete overhaul of the pen in the spring to check for damage incurred over the winter and any infestation of microorganisms, and again in the autumn to prepare for the winter. In April and October carry out the following:

➤ Place the rabbit somewhere safe for the next 24 hours.

➤ Completely empty the pen.

➤ Check over the bowl, bottle, hayrack, toys and chews – do any need replacing?

➤ Check over the pen by paying particular attention to
- Security – check all catches and doors;

- Roofing, for waterproofness;
- Wire netting on the door – replace any damaged wire;
- The inside of the pen, checking for damage from either chewing or damp seepage/rot – fix any damage.

➤ Thoroughly scrub the inside of the pen with pet-safe disinfectant.

➤ Using appropriate safety precautions, use a blowtorch to scorch the inside of the pen, paying particular attention to all joints and cracks – this kills off any microorganisms that the disinfectant has missed.

➤ When the pen is thoroughly dry, paint the internal floor with waterproof pet-safe Tarpaint.

➤ Allow the pen to dry overnight so the floor is completely dry before you put new bedding and either new or cleaned equipment back in the pen.

➤ Put the rabbit back in the pen and feed it.

9. Biannual Health Check

Take your rabbit to the veterinarian twice a year for a full checkup.

10. Seasonal Life-Pattern Routine

Just as we close the doors and windows to

keep out the cold during the winter yet throw them wide open for the warmth and fresh air in the summer, so we must make a similar adjustment to how we keep our rabbit, ensuring that it is comfortable and healthy **throughout the year. See pages 50–53 for detailed information.**

Healthy rabbits are happy rabbits.

The proud winner of Best Pet Rabbit.

Local Pet Shows

At local pet shows the judge, who may not be a rabbit specialist, will likely assess the pets presented to them for three qualities:

- Condition,
- Cleanliness,
- Friendliness.

Now this can be extremely difficult for the judge, who may well have to assess rabbits, hamsters, rats, budgies, stick insects and goldfish – in fact, any pet that you can think of – all in the same class. Nevertheless, a good rabbit in great condition that is immaculately clean and shows a bit of character and friendliness toward the judge stands just as good a chance to win as any of the other animals.

Your rabbit does not need to be a pedigree, although it can be, and it does not have to conform to any breed standard or color pattern. In fact, it is often the mismarked rabbits that catch the judge's eye, and one ear up and one down often has an appeal as long as the rabbit is clean and in good condition.

Exhibiting at these shows does require you to train your rabbit (see Training Your Rabbit, pages 100–111), and any prize that you win will reflect how well you have done so.

Generally they are a great day out, especially for children, and preparing the rabbit for the show is a great way to teach children pet responsibility.

Many of the ARBA-supported rabbit shows

Part of the fun of owning a rabbit is taking it to pet or rabbit shows and competing against others people's rabbits. Of course, some people are very competitive and go to shows to win and anything less is a disappointment to them, while other people go for the day out and to be with and talk to people with a kindred interest in rabbits.

There are two types of show where you can exhibit your rabbit – the local pet show and the American Rabbit Breeders Association show – and they are very different.

Children's pet show.

hold a pet show alongside the main event. These pet shows are usually open to anyone and are run on the same lines as the pet shows described above. Because they are held alongside the main show, they are a great window into what really happens at the ARBA-supported shows. Here you

Products are available to prepare your rabbit for the pet show. Nail trimmers, brush and shampoo could all help you get a prize.

will meet and be able to talk to rabbit fanciers, many of whom will have had a lifetime's experience in breeding, raising, keeping and showing rabbits. The ARBA also sponsors youth shows, which are excellent venues for young rabbit fanciers who are just starting out.

American Rabbit Breeders Association Shows

The American Rabbit Breeders Association (ARBA) is the governing body for rabbit breeders and exhibitors in the United States and Canada. It began as the National Pet Stock Association in 1910 and became the American Rabbit and Cavy Breeders Association in 1923. The name was shortened in 1952 to the American Rabbit Breeders Association, although it continues to be dedicated to the promotion, development and improvement of both rabbits and cavies.

The association is divided into nine districts, which cover the United States and Canada from Alaska to Hawaii, also taking in Japan and Puerto Rico. The ARBA is headquarted in Bloomington, Indiana.

The ARBA has an official magazine called *Domestic Rabbits*, which is mailed to members every other month. This useful publication includes details of upcoming shows and events, rabbit (and cavy) news from around the United States and Canada, articles from veterinarians and rabbit fanciers, market reports and more. The ARBA website also has a number of books and guides available from its online store, including its *Standard of Perfection*.

The spoils of victory.

In addition, the ARBA's Hall of Fame Library in Bloomington, Indiana, is the world's largest single collection of rabbit and cavy publications in the world. ARBA members, visitors and researchers can visit the library to view and study the collection, but the library's holdings are not loaned out.

The ARBA can be contacted through its official website, www.arba.net, and rabbit fanciers can locate their district by visiting www.arba.net/Districts.htm.

To exhibit rabbits at an ARBA-supported show you must first be a fully paid-up member of the ARBA, and your rabbit must be legibly marked in the left ear (see Ear Number, page 59). Legibility of the ear mark is at the discretion of the judge.

All rabbits exhibited under the ARBA rules must be pedigrees (purebred) and must conform as closely as possible to the standard required for its breed, outlined in the *Standard of Perfection*, as well as a list of general requirements relating to health and condition. This may all sound somewhat daunting, but the *Oxford Dictionary* definition of "fancier," "the art or practice of breeding animals so as to develop particular points," sheds some light on the situation. In other words, rabbit fanciers are continually striving to breed rabbits that more closely resemble the required breed standard rather than characteristics that are pleasing in only a general way or conform to a different breed's standard.

In addition to the ARBA, many breeds also have their own specialty clubs, which may also organize their own sweepstakes and shows, separate from the ARBA. However, these clubs also occasionally "sanction" ARBA shows, meaning points awarded at the ARBA show will also count toward awards given out by the sanctioning club. A list of clubs can be found at the ARBA's website, at www.arba.net/National%20Clubs.htm.

Anyone interested in taking up the "rabbit habit" and becoming a fancier would be advised to visit a couple of ARBA-supported rabbit shows first to see what they are like and if it really is for them. All upcoming shows are listed on the ARBA website (www.arba.net/Shows.php).

LEFT A successful day's showing.

Judging at a show.

10 • Training Your Rabbit

What do you want your rabbit to be?

→ House pet/companion.

→ Pen/yard pet.

→ Pet plus local pet/rabbit shows.

→ ARBA-supported show rabbit.

The training your rabbit needs to meet the requirements of each of these roles is slightly different, although there is one basic requirement no matter what you intend to do with your rabbit: it must learn to be sociable and easy to handle, although even the level of sociability will vary with the rabbit's role. You do not want a show rabbit climbing up the judge's shoulder for "kisses," which may be acceptable behavior for a pet, but most certainly is not on the show bench.

Training a Rabbit as a House Pet/Companion

→ Socializing – start handling early; little and often is the answer as young rabbits, like young children, tire quickly. Do not overwhelm the young rabbit; if you sit on the floor the rabbit's natural inquisitiveness will bring it to you so you can stroke it and allow it to climb onto you. It will soon learn to associate you with kindness and the caring attention that all rabbits seek.

Even a house rabbit should have a secure bed area that it can be shut into for safety while you are sleeping or are out of the house. They learn from a very young age that their bed is their safe area. You are certainly not doing them any favors by leaving them out in a hostile environment while you are not there to supervise them.

Start socializing early – little and often.

Sharing the yard.

A commercial brand of rabbit chew that will help your rabbit to exercise its natural desire to chew, discouraging it from damaging objects in the home.

✦ Start litter training early in the rabbit's life – it comes quite naturally to most rabbits and will make your life easier and your house cleaner the quicker it learns. Do not shout at or hit a rabbit. This will not help to train them and will just scare them. Kindness and patience are what work.

✦ Fact – rabbits chew! Protect your wires, behind the TV, telephone, etc., in plastic tubing. If a rabbit chews furniture or wallpaper, spray bitter apple or a similar product so that it tastes bitter to the rabbit and it learns not to chew – again, shouting or hitting do not work.

✦ If you find your rabbit attacks one particular member of the family it is usually scent related. It may be a perfume, a particular soap or hand cream or even an aftershave that the rabbit has taken a dislike to. Some trial and error should soon isolate what it is that the rabbit does not like, and harmony can be restored in the household.

✦ It is worth taking a young rabbit for a few short trips in the car in a secure, well-ventilated box. This teaches it that it will come home again, and then when it does have to go in the car, to the vet or on vacation, it is far less stressful for it.

TIP How to pick your rabbit up

1 Have the rabbit facing you on a firm surface. Grasp the ears firmly with one hand, the other hand cupping the rump.

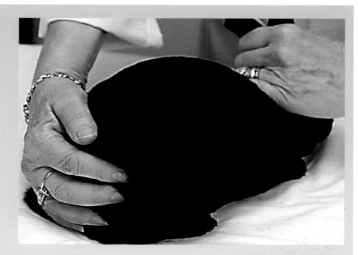

2 Lift from the back so the rabbit's weight is supported in one palm while the other hand steadies the head by holding the ears.

3 Clasp the rabbit to your chest, supporting the weight with one hand and placing the other hand on its back. The rabbit will feel secure in this position.

Training a Pen/Yard Pet

You may think that a rabbit that lives in a pen in the yard needs little or no training, but perhaps the socializing of a yard-kept rabbit is more important than that of a house rabbit. The pen rabbit will not have as much contact with you and the rest of the family as one living in the house would have, but you do not want to be attacked when you go near the pen.

- Socializing must start early – little and often. Remember that rabbits like to sleep in the afternoon, so try to hold your training session either in the early morning or in the evening.

- Get your young rabbit used to being picked up and held every time you come to the pen.

- Give them plenty of toys, gnawing blocks and general distractions to stop them from becoming bored and frustrated during the periods they are on their own.

- Try to get them used to having a litter tray in the corner of their pen from an early age. This will make your life a lot easier in the years to come.

- It is worth taking a young pen rabbit for a few short trips in the car in a secure, well-ventilated box. This teaches them that

Rabbits sleep in the afternoon.

Get them used to being turned over in your lap. It will make nail cutting much easier.

they will come home again, and then when they do have to go in the car, to the vet or on vacation, it is far less stressful for them.

➤ Where are you going to put your rabbit when you clean out the pen each week? You may let them have a run, or you may box them. Either way, get them used to a cleaning routine from a young age.

➤ Get them used to being turned over in your lap from a young age. This will make health checks and nail cutting much easier when they are older.

➤ It is quite natural for a doe to get grumpy when she thinks she wants mating; you do have to be careful at times like this, especially with young children – rabbit bites are really nasty and quite frightening. Use a shovel or dustpan to distract them (let them attack it) while you grab the food bowl. They will get over it and return to their normal loving selves once the hormones have sorted themselves out.

Training for Local Pet/Rabbit Shows
Obviously your pet rabbit that you wish to show at one of your local pet shows will require training.

At most pet shows the judge will be assessing your rabbit based on three qualities: condition, cleanliness and friendliness.

There is little training you can do to ensure the conditioning of your rabbit, other than training yourself to feed your rabbit correctly and to keep it in an airy environment that promotes a healthy coat covering a fit, muscular body.

You can, however, train your rabbit from a very early age to allow you to groom it; this may even include washing its feet. A judge really does expect your rabbit to be clean. You cannot take a dirty rabbit with stained feet and an unkempt coat and make it presentable overnight.

Regular grooming should get the coat in order, but perhaps the hardest part of preparing a pet rabbit for a show is getting its feet clean. Running free in the garden or yard is out for a couple of weeks before the show. Clean bedding, which you must keep changing and keep clean, is a necessity, and some serious feet cleaning is in order. If your rabbit is used to lying on its back on your lap and having its feet handled your task will be much easier. You can scrub (gently) your rabbit's feet using an old toothbrush and soap; dry the rabbit's feet and place it in a clean pen. If the feet are badly stained you may have to do this a few times in the weeks before the show.

Your training for friendliness should of course have started at a very early age, but the difference if you wish to show the rabbit is that it has to be friendly to whoever handles

Show rabbits must be trained to sit in their breed's recognized pose.

it and not just to you. You should therefore try to let different people turn your rabbit over and generally pet it.

Although pet rabbits are not expected to sit in the pose of a show rabbit, it does help if they will sit peacefully and at ease on the judge's table. You can train your rabbit by having a "show table" at home, where you can train your rabbit to sit at ease. Much of this type of training is down to the way that you handle your rabbit; if you handle it in a quiet, confident manner your rabbit will be calm and relaxed – just how you want it for the judge's table.

Training a Rabbit for American Rabbit Breeders Association (ARBA) Supported Shows

To enter an ARBA-supported rabbit show you must be a paid-up member of the ARBA, and your rabbit must have an ear number in its left ear (see page 59). Your rabbit must be purebred and conform to the standard for the breed outlined in the ARBA *Standard of Perfection*. If you and your rabbit meet these requirements you will still need to spend a considerable amount of time training and preparing your rabbit for the show.

Show rabbits should be kept in pens:
- Sunlight ruins the color of the coat,
- Yards stain feet,
- Yards are full of dangers that can damage your rabbit.

Show rabbits must be kept in scrupulously clean conditions.

Show rabbits must be trained to sit in the required pose for the breed. This will be required for lengthy periods at some shows, and they could be on the judge's table for as long as half an hour. Build a show bench at home where you can train your show rabbit from an early age. Little and often is the only way to go; do not allow your rabbit to climb up onto you, but hold it gently in the required pose and smooth it down the back with the palm of your hand. When it starts to fidget and has clearly had enough of sitting do some grooming.

Your show rabbit will be expected to be in perfect condition and spotlessly clean. The judge will turn it over on its back to check that it is, so get it used to being turned over and having its feet and legs touched. The judge will also check your rabbit's teeth, so, again, get it used to this simple and painless procedure – if you are not sure how to do it yourself ask an experienced fancier to show you.

The standards required of show rabbits are exacting, and the only way you can possibly get your rabbit up to this standard is by careful and diligent husbandry and continual training, that is, training for a short spell almost every day.

Show rabbits must be spotlessly clean.

The author takes Best in Show with a young English Lop at an agricultural show.

ARBA Show Rules

The Official Show Rules of the American Rabbit Breeders Association, Inc., outlines how points are awarded and provides codes of conducts for exhibitors, judges and show organizers.

Points are awarded for the top five rabbits in each class. First prize counts as six points, second counts as four, third counts as three, fourth counts as two and fifth counts as one point. The number of points won by the rabbit is then calculated by multiplying the number of animals exhibited and judged in the class by the number of point being counted. As such, if 10 rabbits from the fur class are competing, the animal that places first will win 60 points, and the animal that places fifth will receive 10 points.

Awards for Best of Breed, Best Opposite Sex of Breed, Best of Group, Best Opposite Sex of Group, Best of Variety and Best Opposite Sex of Variety are given, as applicable. Additional awards can include Best Junior, Best Intermediate and Best Senior.

There is always an award for Best Rabbit in Show. When judging the Best in Show, each Best of Breed is brought back to the judging table for comparison – Best in Show is not judged by highest total of points.

Rabbits are not officially entered until all required fees are paid, which must be done prior to the start of the show. In the event only one rabbit is competing in a class, the judge will award the animal a first if he or she considers that it would have placed in good competition. Otherwise the animal is noted as being "unworthy of an award."

Substitutions may be accepted at the discretion of the show sponsor. However, no substitutions, changes or additions are allowed after judging of the breed has begun, and an animal can only be substituted with one of the same sex, class, variety, group and breed.

Chartered clubs must accept all breeds recognized in the ARBA *Standard of Perfection*, but national, state and local specialty clubs can only accept the breed or breeds they sponsor. Every animal must be exhibited in its natural condition and cannot be dyed, plucked, trimmed or otherwise altered. Animals that violate this rule will be disqualified, and any other animals belonging to the offending exhibitor may also be disqualified.

Exhibitors have the right to protest a judge's decision if their rabbit has placed or was wrongfully disqualified or if they allege fraud on the part of a judge. Protests must be made in writing within two hours of awards being placed. A fee must be paid, but it will be refunded if the protest is upheld. In the case of a protest being upheld, the awards are adjusted accordingly.

Anyone interested in exhibiting their rabbits should consult the full text of the show rules, which can be obtained from the ARBA website, at http://www.arba.net/Forms.htm.

PART THREE

The Rabbit Breeds

11 • The Fancy Breeds

Fancy rabbits are an odd collection of exhibition rabbits. Fur rabbits are bred for their fur, lop rabbits for their lop ears and rex animals for their lustrous, smooth coats. The only thing that unites the fancy rabbits is that they have no other use than exhibition.

Many of the fancy breeds are, in fact, very old and have survived the vagaries of time. Individual breeds come and go in popularity, depending on the trends.

In the past, the wool of the Angora rabbit has been much sought after and highly prized. For many years, Belgian Hares were exported to the United States in vast numbers, often fetching phenomenal sums.

Currently it would appear that the little Red-eyed White Pole is much in demand as a show winner, while the popularity of the Lionhead, not yet recognized by the ARBA, is very much in the ascendancy.

It is the diversity of the fancy rabbits that is the strength of this section, which is a truly wonderful collection of breeds that surely has something for everybody.

Blue Dutch

Angora

The Angora is a highly specialized rabbit that has been bred throughout history for its wool. Its long, silky hair is akin to that of the Angora goat, after which it is named. It is a very ancient breed that may well have been kept by the Romans but always for that one purpose – its wool. Whole industries have developed around the wool of the Angora rabbit, which should not be confused with that of the Angora goat. At the beginning of the 19th century in the Savoy area of France, a whole industry sprung up, hand spinning angora wool into gloves and undergarments that were light and very warm.

Two strains of Angora have been developed: the French, which is a larger animal and has a coat described as "as long as possible, soft and silky and extremely dense"; and the smaller English Angora, with a coat described as "as silky as possible, even and full all over." The Angora is unique in that its coat is multilayered.

Chinchilla Angora

The tips of each new coat are darker than the previous coat, which lightens as it gains length. This produces a banding effect in the coat.

Due to the length of their coat and the special attention it requires, Angoras are not suitable as pets.

Pet Suitability	None
Good Points	For exhibition only
Poor Points	Coat requires constant care
Weight	About 7 lb. (3.2 kg)
Colours	White plus a range of colors special to breed
Keep in	Pen, cage

*Red-eyed White
English Angora*

Belgian Hare

The first thing to say about the Belgian Hare is that it is not a hare. It is a rabbit that closely resembles a wild hare, and originally it had very similar coloring. A true hare lives aboveground rather than burrowing like a rabbit, and it gives birth to furred young that have their eyes open, unlike the bald, blind young of the rabbit.

Although originating in the Flanders area of Belgium, it was when the Belgian Hare was brought to England in 1874 that it created a major impact on the rabbit world, firstly in Britain and later in the U.S., both as an exhibition and a meat rabbit.

Often described as the racehorse of the rabbit family, the graceful Belgian Hare has a long, streamlined body that arches from the shoulders to the tail. The front legs are particularly long and slender. The Hare's fur lies close to its body and is rather harsh in texture, but it is the color of a fit Belgian Hare that is most striking. To say that it looks stunning is without a doubt an understatement – maybe spectacular describes it better.

Tan Belgian Hare

Pet Suitability	✶✶✶✶
Good Points	Amenable nature
Poor Points	Quite delicate when young
Weight	8–9 lb. (3.6–4 kg)
Colours	Rich, deep chestnut, red (whites and tans are now being introduced)
Keep in	Pen, cage

In recent years there has been a move by a few dedicated rabbit fanciers to introduce a White Belgian Hare (with red eyes) and a black and tan-colored one. On the show bench "type" is always more important than color, so if the breeders of these new colors can produce Hares in red-eyed white or black and tan that have just as good a type as the traditional chestnut red ones, it may not be long before we see the new colors taking top honors at the shows. Whether either of the new breeds catches on remains to be seen.

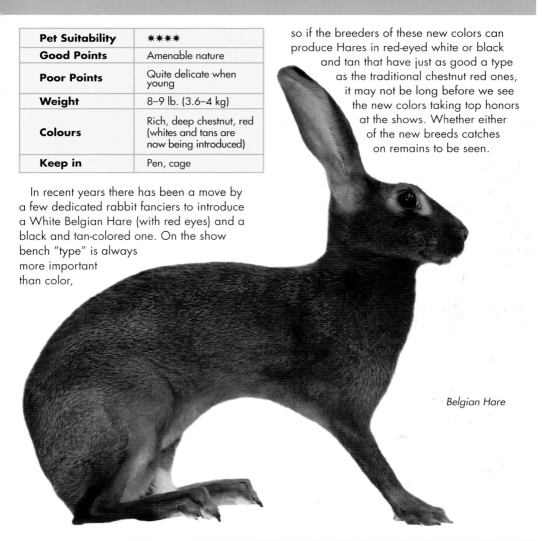

Belgian Hare

119

Dutch

The Dutch is an extremely popular rabbit that is ideal for the beginner or for any young rabbit owner. The ease with which the Dutch will settle into any situation makes it an ideal pet to live either in a pen or in the house.

Black Dutch

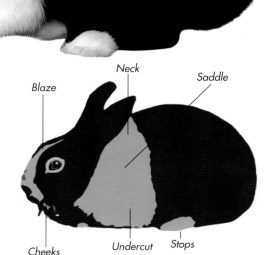

Because of their compact size and robust nature, they adapt readily to being handled, even by the inexperienced, and thus readily endear themselves to their human companion.

Dutch does are renowned as good mothers and are often kept by fanciers to be used as foster mothers, sometimes for quite large breeds. It is not uncommon to see a little Dutch doe raising a litter of rabbits as large as English Lops in a fancier's shed.

One of the big attractions of the Dutch rabbit

Pet Suitability	★★★★★
Good Points	Temperament, size, hardiness
Poor Points	None
Weight	4½ lb. (2.3 kg)
Colors	Black, blue, yellow, chocolate, tortoiseshell, gray
Keep In	Pen, cage, yard, house

Blaze • Neck • Saddle • Cheeks • Undercut • Stops

The markings of the Dutch rabbit.

Tort Dutch

Yellow Dutch

to the fancy exhibitor is its markings or, rather, the delineation between its markings (i.e. the clean lines between the colors). The inheritance of the markings is genetic, and, therefore, the fancier can employ skill and knowledge to try to breed the perfect specimen. Of course, there is no such thing as the perfect specimen, but many a fancier has made it their life's work to try and breed as near a perfect Dutch as possible. Some have come very close.

The markings on a Dutch rabbit have a language of their own; saddle, blaze, stops, undercut and cheeks are the terms frequently heard when the Dutch rabbit is being judged.

English

The English is the ultimate never-say-die rabbit of the rabbit world. There is no other exhibition rabbit that so utterly defies the "breeding for perfection" philosophy of the fancy. Besides breeding for shape and color, breeders must strive to achieve the markings, which affect every part of the animal from its nose to its tail. These markings not only have to be in the right position but of a specific shape.

The consequence of the difficulties encountered by breeders trying to achieve

Pet Suitability	★★★★
Good Points	Temperament, hardiness
Poor Points	Size
Weight	6–8 lb. (2.7–3.6 kg)
Colors	Black, blue, chocolate, tortoiseshell, gray
Keep In	Pen, cage, yard, house

Black English with very good markings.

the unachievable is that many English rabbits are sold into the pet trade. But just because a rabbit has a spot or two in the wrong place doesn't mean it will be any less of a wonderful pet companion.

If the size does not deter you (this is quite a big rabbit), then here is a wonderful, robust rabbit that should make a superb pet for either the house or yard.

Black English with poor chain and blurred spots.

The Markings Required of the Exhibition English Rabbit

HEAD MARKINGS
1. Perfect butterfly smut.
2. Circles around eyes.
3. Cheek spots to be clear from eye circles.
4. Ears neat and clear from white.

BODY MARKINGS
1. Unbroken saddle to be herringboned and clear in any distinct color from base of ears to tip of tail.
2. Body, or loin, markings to be nicely broken up and not to catch the saddle.
3. Chain markings to be as even as possible on each side.
4. Leg markings one distinct spot on each leg.
5. Belly or teat spots.

Flemish Giant

As the name suggests, the Flemish Giant hails from Belgium, where it was originally a much larger rabbit – does in excess of 21 pounds (9.5 kg) were not uncommon. Today, exhibition does are usually between 12 and 14 pounds (5.4–6.3 kg).

Here is a large rabbit that will need a lot of quite careful feeding; plenty of excellent food for growth when young, and then a good stable diet as an adult that keeps the rabbit in good shape

Pet Suitability	★★★★
Good Points	Temperament, hardiness
Poor Points	Size
Weight	Not less than 11 lb. bucks/12 lb. does (5 kg/5.4 kg)
Colors	Dark steel gray
Keep In	Pen, yard

Dark Steel Gray Flemish Giant

Giant Papillon
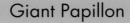

and does not allow it to become overweight. Overweight rabbits are just as likely to fall prey to obesity-related maladies as humans are, and considerable willpower is required to regulate the adult Flemish Giant's diet.

It is not uncommon for self blacks to appear in litters; however, because exhibition Flemish Giants are required to be dark steel-gray, those blacks are usually sold on by the breeders to become pets, and excellent pets they can make if you have the space for such a large rabbit.

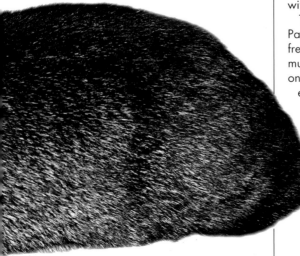

Pet Suitability	★★★
Good Points	Temperament, hardiness
Poor Points	Size
Weight	Over 11 lb. (5 kg)
Colors	Base color is white with any recognized color markings
Keep In	Pen, yard, house

This is one of the giant rabbits that may well weigh 13 to14 pounds (over 6 kg). But for its size it has a fairly fine-boned skeleton, unlike the French Lop, which is of comparable size but has a heavy bone structure. The Giant Papillon carries most of its immense weight in muscle; the front of the rabbit is very well developed, with a large muscled chest and shoulders.

The most important feature of the Giant Papillon is of course its butterfly (*papillon* is french for butterfly) smut nose markings. These must be well defined, with the two wings full on both sides and only lightly touching the edges of the lower jaw.

You are unlikely to find Giant Papillions for sale in a pet store and would have to contact a specialist breeder if you think they could be the breed for you.

Harlequin and Magpie

If breeding English rabbits for the correct markings defines the concept of breeding for perfection, then breeding the Harlequin or Magpie for the show bench is surely just as demanding.

The difference between the Harlequin and the Magpie is simply color combinations. To simplify this, let us consider the Black Harlequin, which is a combination of golden orange and dense black.

The head should be equally divided, with one half black and the other golden orange, with a clear definition

line. There should be one black ear on the orange side of the face and an orange one on the black side. There should be one front leg orange, while the other should be black. Similarly, one hind leg should be orange and the other black, but reversed from the combination

Pet Suitability	✷✷✷✷
Good Points	Temperament, hardiness
Poor Points	Size
Weight	6–8 lb. (2.7–3.6 kg)
Colors	See opposite
Keep In	Pen, yard, house

Orange and black Harlequin

Harlequin and Magpie Colors

Black Harlequin: Dense black and golden orange.
Blue Harlequin: Lavender blue and golden fawn.
Brown Harlequin: Rich, dark brown and golden orange.
Lilac Harlequin: Dove gray and golden fawn.
Black Magpie: Dense black and white.
Blue Magpie: Lavender blue and white.
Brown Magpie: Rich, dark brown and white.
Lilac Magpie: Dove gray and white.

at the front. As if that were not enough, the body should be banded in black and orange, and the bands should be clearly defined.

From the description of the markings required for a show Harlequin, it is obvious that many examples of the breed will not come up to this very demanding standard. As a result, it is quite common to see them for sale in pet stores, and they make very fine pets indeed.

*White and black
Magpie*

Himalayan

*Himalayan Normal
(black points)*

The Himalayan is a very old variety of rabbit, believed to have originated in Asia. It is an elegant, and somewhat delicate, little rabbit whose body type is described as snaky. Its coat is always white in color and is short and very fine. This all adds to the slight appearance of the rabbit.

Strangely, Himalayans are born all white and do not gain their colored points until they are about three months old. It is producing a rabbit with good depth of color in the points that is the breeder's main challenge. The colored markings on the legs are known as stockings.

Himis are notoriously docile, passive little rabbits, which of course can be an advantage

Pet Suitability	****
Good Points	Temperament, size
Poor Points	Hardiness
Weight	About 4½ lb. (2 kg)
Colors	White with points in black, blue, chocolate or lilac
Keep in	Pen

if you want a rabbit that will be easy to handle, but it's a bit of a disappointment if you want a little character who will entertain you.

Lionhead

The Lionhead is the new star of the rabbit world, officially recognized by the BRC in 2002. It is not yet by the ARBA, although it has been presented at shows, and a standard is being developed. It is fair to say that this cobby little rabbit with a mane like an African lion has taken the rabbit world, on both sides of the Atlantic, by storm.

Being the same size as the Holland Lop, the Lionhead does not require large accommodation or a great deal of food. It is very easily kept and is very adaptable to almost any situation. It is little wonder that the breed has become so popular.

Of course, as with any new trend, there will always be those who exploit the situation. There are plenty of Lionheads being bred for the pet market, but be careful and check the rabbit you are buying very carefully. Do not allow your heart to rule your head. Most breeders are dedicated to producing good, healthy stock but there are always some that will spoil things with irresponsible breeding.

Baby Lionheads tend to have an excess of

*Red-eyed
White
Lionhead*

Pet Suitability	★★★★★
Good Points	Temperament, size, character
Poor Points	None
Weight	3–3½ lb. (1.4–1.6 kg.)
Colors	All ARBA-recognized colors
Keep In	Pen, cage, house, yard

"furnishings" i.e. too much long hair all over their heads and bodies. As adults, they should have a mane of between 2 and 3 inches (5–8 cm), forming a full circle around the head and falling to a fringe between the ears. They will have noticeably longer hair on the cheeks and chest but should not have a skirt (long hair around the back end). This staged development makes it extremely difficult for the breeder or exhibitor to select the right babies to keep and those to let go. If you do wind up with a Lionhead that has long hair all around its body, it is going to require significantly more grooming than one that only has a long mane.

Young Lionhead

Adult Lionhead with a good mane.

Netherland Dwarf

The Netherland Dwarf, as the name suggests, is the smallest recognized breed of rabbit. It is extremely popular with rabbit exhibitors because it requires little space, is cheap to keep and offers the breeder an endless variety of colors and patterns to work on. However, while it can be trained to show itself off on the show bench, it is its temperament that has diminished its popularity as a pet. It is very easy to fall into the trap of believing this Lilliputian breed will be docile and compliant, but it may well not be. For all its diminutive size, the Netherland Dwarf can inflict a very nasty bite when it decides to do so. Of course, there are many Netherland Dwarfs living happy, contented lives as pets, but it must not automatically be assumed that this will be the case. Perhaps some kind of money-back guarantee should be arranged with the seller at the time of purchase in case things don't work out.

Adult Marten Sable Netherland Dwarf

Dwarf Blue Otter

REW Netherland Dwarf

The Netherland Dwarf is short, compact, cobby and wide at the shoulders, not racy. The front legs should be short, straight and fine in bone. Ears should be well furred, slightly rounded at the tips but not necessarily touching and 2 inches (5 cm) in length. The head is round with a broad skull. The eyes are round, bold and bright. The fur is soft and dense.

Agouti Netherland Dwarf

Pet Suitability	✴✴✴
Good Points	Size, cost of keeping
Poor Points	Temperament can be suspect
Weight	2–2½ lb. (0.9–1.1 kg)
Colors	All ARBA-recognized colors
Keep In	Pen, cage

Polish

The Polish is a neat, compact little bantam weight of a rabbit that differs from the Netherland Dwarf in that its features are quite fine, even delicate. It is a sprightly little rabbit that is known as the showman of the fancy, and it has probably won more top honors at shows over the years than any other breed of rabbit.

But among many novice exhibitors, the Pole is feared and avoided. Poles must be handled correctly, or they will let you know in no uncertain way – with their teeth!

The colored Poles seem to have a more placid nature than the whites, but, as a whole, the breed is best left in the hands of experienced exhibitors.

Smoke Pearl Pole – colored Poles are usually more placid than the whites.

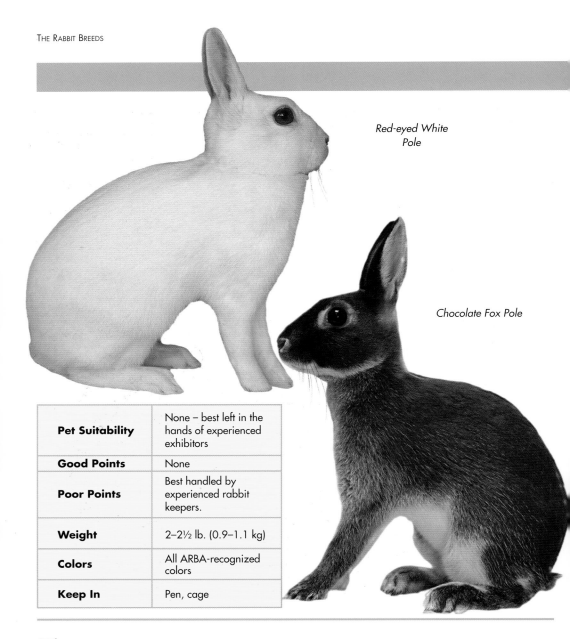

Red-eyed White
Pole

Chocolate Fox Pole

Pet Suitability	None – best left in the hands of experienced exhibitors
Good Points	None
Poor Points	Best handled by experienced rabbit keepers.
Weight	2–2½ lb. (0.9–1.1 kg)
Colors	All ARBA-recognized colors
Keep In	Pen, cage

Silver

The Silver Gray is a very old breed that was originally a warren rabbit (i.e., it was kept in rabbit warrens and cropped for its valuable fur). The breed was first known as the Lincolnshire Sprig, from which it is logical to conclude that it was bred in that part of England. It has been bred for exhibition since about 1860.

Silvers are very attractive rabbits. They are also lively and bright in disposition, making them ideal companion pets. This is a very adaptable breed that requires no special treatment.

Silvers come in four colors: black (called gray), brown (a deep, rich chestnut), fawn (a deep, bright orange) and blue (a dark slate blue). The base color is covered with silvering or ticking, which should be as even as possible over all parts of the rabbit.

Pet Suitability	★★★★
Good Points	Size, temperament, easy to keep, very adaptable
Poor Points	None
Weight	5–6 lb. (2.3–2.7 kg)
Colors	Silver gray, silver fawn, silver brown, silver blue
Keep In	Pen, cage, house or yard. Show Silvers must be kept indoors to retain their color

Gray Silver

For the breeder and exhibitor, the depth of the base color and the evenness of the ticking (the silvering that covers the base color) are important. This means that many animals that do not meet these exacting requirements find their way into the pet trade.

When the young Silvers first fur-up (at about 12 days old) they are just their base color (black, blue, brown or fawn). They do not start to silver until they are about five weeks old. If the silvering appears first at the toes and then spreads up across the whole body there is a good chance of the all-important even ticking. However, if he silvering first appears at the

nose and then spreads downward, it is highly unlikely that there will be sufficient ticking left for the toes. Unfortunately for the breeder or exhibitor, the silvering process is not likely to be completed until the youngsters are some three to four months old. It is not until this point that they can tell whether the young Silver is going to be suitable for showing or should go to the pet store.

Fawn Silver

Tan

The Tan is a very old breed that originated from an unknown cross in a rabbit warren. The base color (black, blue, chocolate or lilac) has rich tan-colored markings. The eye circles, nostrils, jowls, chest, belly, flanks and underside of the tail should be a solid mass of deep, golden tan. With its fairly short, silky coat lying close to its body, a fit, young Black Tan is a truly magnificent sight.

Tans that are being exhibited need to be kept in an inside rabbitry, as the effect of direct sunlight on their coats degenerates the all-important color. But a pet Tan is a most adaptable rabbit that will readily adjust to any clean, warm, draft-free living space.

Tans are exceptionally easy rabbits to keep. They require no special food, housing or special treatment. Added to their generally amenable nature, this makes them an ideal pet.

Breeders of Tans mix the colors to improve depth and richness of shade, so it is quite likely that an exceptional black buck will be mated

Black Tan

to a blue doe. The breeder would hope the richness of the blue in any blue offspring would be improved, and the offspring would carry the father's exceptional type while the effect of the blue mother on any black youngsters in the litter would be to help increase the depth of black down the hair shaft. It is desirable for the color to reach right down the hair shaft to the skin, but sometimes the base of the hair shaft can become light (or even white). These are the kinds of minor points that top breeders are working to improve in their line (i.e., their successive generations of stock).

Pet Suitability	★★★★★
Good Points	Size, temperament, easy to keep, very adaptable
Poor Points	None
Weight	4½ lb. (2 kg)
Colors	Black and tan, blue and tan, chocolate and tan, lilac and tan
Keep In	Pen, cage, house or yard; show Tans must be kept indoors to retain their color

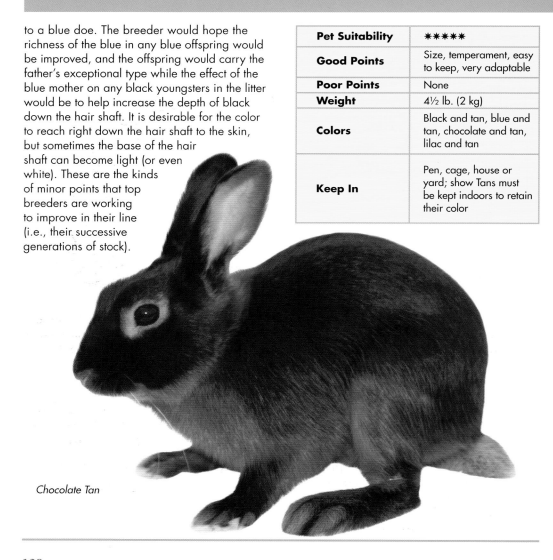

Chocolate Tan

Thrianta

Thrianta

With its beautifully dense, soft close coat, the Thrianta feels as if it should be in the fur section. However, when the Breeds Standard Committee of the British Rabbit Council accepted the Thrianta they placed it with the fancy rabbits, and there it has stayed. The Thrianta is also considered a fancy breed by the American Rabbit Breeders Association.

The Thrianta is a firm, cobby, robust, mid-sized rabbit that is probably best kept outdoors to allow an ample dose of fresh air to work on the coat. A Thrianta that is kept indoors is not likely to ever clear its coat of molt and will therefore never achieve the wonderfully lustrous, rich reddish golden coat that the breed is known for.

The Thrianta is a rare breed, and anyone seeking one as a pet would probably be best to contact the American Thrianta Rabbit Breeders Association.

Pet Suitability	✶✶✶✶✶
Good Points	Size, temperament, easy to keep, very adaptable
Poor Points	Rare breed – hard to find
Weight	4½–6 lb. (2–2.7 kg)
Colors	Bright intense reddish golden)
Keep In	Pen, yard

12 • The Lop Breeds

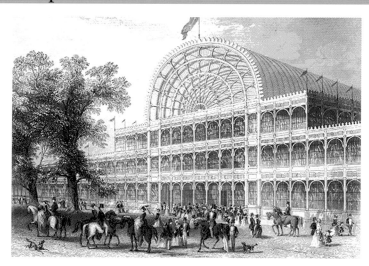

An English Lop won at the Great Exhibition show held at Crystal Palace, London, England, in 1851.

In recent years, the understanding of the science behind breeding and inheritance has been a driving force behind the development of new lop breeds, but it is still worth considering where the original lop-eared rabbit came from.

How did we get from the wild rabbit that weighed about 3 pounds (2.5 kg) with upright ears that measured a mere 7½ inches (19 cm) from tip to tip and just 1⅞ inches (5 cm) wide to the English Lop that can weigh as much as 20 pounds (9 kg) and can have ears measuring up to 30 inches (76 cm) long and 7½ inches (19 cm) wide?

To understand the extraordinary development of lops we must look briefly at the domestication

of the wild rabbit. We know from ancient records that the domestication of the wild rabbit started with the Romans, who took rabbits on board their ships in cages as a ready source of fresh meat for the armies they were transporting.

After the Romans, monks perpetuated the keeping of rabbits in cages for many centuries. Using cages or rabbit courts (which are sometimes known as rabbit gardens), monks could have a ready supply of meat for all those living in the monastery. The keeping of rabbits in enclosed spaces had two major effects. It caused the captive rabbits to become large and lazy, as they did not have to run from their predators. But, perhaps more importantly,

Crystal Palace winning lop, 1887.

they also did not need to use their ears to listen out for danger. The result of this enforced captivity was that the rabbits became bigger and the muscles in their heads that had held their ears erect became unused. When these two effects (increased size and lack of ear muscles) are added to the fact that these captive rabbits were being kept in a sheltered environment, away from the chilling effects of the wind, it explains why they became increasingly large animals with ears that drooped in the heat.

At the beginning of the 19th century some enterprising individuals from the East End of London saw how these tame, captive-bred

rabbits could be used to turn a profit. Selective breeding could increase their ear size so that the animals could be exhibited for prize money and bets wagered on the length of their ears. This program of selective breeding, which took place over the first half of the 19th century, effectively created the Lop exhibition rabbit. This animal very closely resembled the English Lop rabbit that we know today.

All current breeds of lop-eared rabbit have been developed from the English Lop, which is now known as the King of the Fancy.

The Cashmere Lop

The Cashmere Lop is a sturdy medium-sized rabbit with a massive head and solid, strong shoulders, that is characterized by its long coat. It has a very similar amenable nature to its cousin the Mini Lop.

Seal Point Cashmere Lop

The first long-haired Cashmere Lops almost certainly appeared as mutants in litters of Mini Lops. The British Rabbit Council recognized the breed under the name of Cashmere Lop in the mid 1980s. The Breed is not recognized by the ARBA. Of course, the rabbit does not produce cashmere wool, but its fine, soft fur strongly resembles that of the cashmere goat from which genuine cashmere wool comes.

Cashmere Lops can be kept in pens, although if traditional wood shavings are used as bedding they can cause considerable problems as they become entangled in the long coat. Many exhibition specimens are kept in wire-floored cages. These have the added advantage of increased ventilation when the weather is

Red-eyed White Cashmere Lop

really hot, but the wire floor can cause sore hocks, in which case the lop should be moved back to a solid wooden-floored pen.

The Cashmere Lop is best left in the hands of the experienced breeder/exhibitor.

Grooming Cashmere and Miniature Cashmere Lops

To keep the Cashmere Lop's long coat in a mat-free condition takes considerable time and effort. Daily grooming sessions must start while the lop is still an adolescent. At this time, when the coat

Sable Mini Cashmere Lop

is particularly wayward, a 10-minute a day grooming session will not only get on top of the developing coat but also accustom the lop to what is going to become a feature of its daily routine.

The Miniature Cashmere Lop

As the Cashmere Lop is a long-haired version of the Mini Lop so the charming little Miniature Cashmere Lop, weighing no more than 3½ pounds (1.6 kg), is the long-haired version of the Holland Lop (also known as the Miniature Lop). The rise in popularity of the Holland Lop throughout the 1990s caused the development of the Miniature Cashmere Lop to be somewhat prolonged, so that it was not recognized by the British Rabbit Council until 2000. It is yet not recognized by the ARBA.

The Miniature Cashmere Lop has the same housing and grooming requirements as the standard Cashmere Lop, and it too is best left in the hands of experienced breeders and exhibitors.

Pet Suitability	**
Good Points	Size, temperament
Poor Points	Coat requires constant care
Weight	4–5½ lb.(2.2–2.4 kg) Mini Cashmere Lops not to exceed 3½ lb. (1.6 kg)
Colors	All ARBA-recognized colors
Keep In	Pen, cage

Red-eyed White Mini Cashmere Lop

Mini Lop

The Mini Lop must surely be the ideal rabbit; of medium size, this robust rabbit is easy to keep and demands little apart from a clean, warm, draft-free bed, its daily rations and a lot of affection from its owner.

Although the Mini Lop was first exhibited in Holland in the 1950s, it did not arrive in the United States until the 1970s, and it was 1980 before the Mini Lop was accepted as a breed by the ARBA.

Also known as the Klein (little) Widder (hanging ears), the Mini Lop has inherited the characteristic features that we now recognize from its ancestors. It inherited its superb dense coat from the Chinchilla, and its multitude of different colors comes from the Netherland Dwarf.

Red-eyed White Dwarf Lop

The Mini Lop is perfectly happy to run free in the house or yard. They make extremely affectionate pets, and keeping them healthy and happy will result in endless hours of fun, love and affection. They can be comical little characters as they toss their toys around and leap gleefully in the air, and they show real enjoyment in the company of their owners.

Sooty Fawn Dwarf Lop

Grooming the Mini Lop

Throughout most of the year, a damp hand rubbed through the coat from the tail toward the head is sufficient to remove any loose hair and keep your Mini Lop's coat beautiful and shiny. But during periods of molt, these rabbits need more serious attention.

During late summer, rabbits shed their summer coat (molt) and grow a thick winter coat to keep them warm in the colder months. Their hair literally falls out by the handful, and, quite frankly, they look awful. You can aid this process by daily grooming with a brush and comb (while being extremely careful not to tear the rabbit's very thin skin). A rubber brush designed for grooming cats is very useful for removing hair from a molting rabbit.

Pet Suitability	★★★★★
Good Points	Size, temperament
Poor Points	None, although as for all flat-faced lops watch teeth
Weight	4½–5½ lb. (1.9–2.4 kg)
Colors	All ARBA-recognized colors
Keep in	Pen, house, shed, yard

English Lop

Agouti Butterfly English Lop

The English Lop, which is characterized by its huge ears, is a very big rabbit that is probably best kept in the hands of experienced fanciers. The King of the Fancy, as the English Lop is known, was first exhibited in London in 1840. The breed has been through many ups and downs since then. Currently, the breed is thriving in the United States while it is quite rare in Britain.

The English Lop has a wonderful nature. If it is kept as a house rabbit it will take on many doglike characteristics: sleeping on the sofa, coming and going through a dog flap in the door, and following its owner around the house. Like a dog, it will also come to dote upon its owner. However, it is not particularly keen on being picked up, and it can give a very big kick to anyone trying to force it to do something it does not want to do.

As a show rabbit it is unequalled. If the English Lop is kept correctly and prepared correctly for showing there is no finer rabbit placed before the judge. Unfortunately, presenting an English Lop in this perfect condition is not easy, and it takes a lot of hard work and dedication.

So although the English Lop is a wonderful rabbit in many ways, it should really only be kept by an experienced pet owner or exhibitor.

Pet Suitability	★★★
Good Points	Temperament
Poor Points	A large rabbit, ears need looking after
Weight	10–12 lb.
	(4.5–5.4 kg)
Colors	REW, black, agouti, fawn, sooty fawn and all in butterfly
Keep In	Pen, house, shed, yard

Judge measuring an English Lop's ear length.

Measuring the English Lop's Ears

Agouti English Lop

When the English Lop is exhibited, the judge measures both the length and breadth of its ears. The judge uses a rigid "yard stick" to measure the ear length from the tip of one ear across the top of the head to the tip of the other ear. Lops must have an ear length in excess of 20 inches (50.5 cm) to be of show standard. Ears measuring 28–30 inches (71–76 cm) by about 7 inches (17.75 cm) are considered excellent. But the lop must still have the characteristic mandolin-shaped body and must conform to the breed standard. It is not just about ears.

German and French Lops

Agouti French Lop

Red-eyed White German Lop

The origins of the French Lop can be traced back to an English Lop that won the Great Exhibition show held at Crystal Palace, London, England, in 1851. This rabbit was exported to Paris, France, where it was cross-mated with Normandy and Flemish Giants. Some of the fledgling French Lops were then exported to Germany, where, because they had come from France, they became known as French Lops. Fanciers in Britain concentrated on the Lop (the English Lop as it was later to become known) and did not import French Lops into England until the 1930s. The French Lop did not become established in the United States until the 1970s.

Orange German Lop

Agouti German Lop

The French Lop is a massive, thickset, cuddly monster of a rabbit that may well weigh in excess of 15 pounds (6.8 kg).

Their placid, laid-back nature makes them ideal pets, especially as house rabbits. Be warned though, they do not necessarily tolerate a dog or cat that attacks them. A French Lop may well attack a cat or dog that has taken liberties with it, and it will often come out the winner.

Although the German Lop is not as big as the French Lop, it is a very solidly built, substantial rabbit. The German Lop was developed to fill the size gap between the Mini Lop and the massive French Lop. It is a highly adaptable rabbit that seems to live quite happily in almost any situation, providing it is kept warm and dry and fed and watered correctly. Although on the large side, the German Lop makes an ideal pet that will return all the love and attention that is lavished on it by its owner.

Neither the French nor German Lops take kindly to being stuck in a pen at the bottom of the yard and being largely ignored. Both breeds crave human contact. A lop that has lots of love and attention will be a contented lop; one that is ignored and deprived of human contact may show aggression.

Pet Suitability	★★★★★
Good Points	Temperament, hardy and robust
Poor Points	Size
Weight	German Lop 6½–8½ lb. (2.9–3.9 kg);
	French Lop over 10 lb. (over 4½ kg)
Colors	All recognized colors
Keep In	Pen, house, shed, yard

Meissner Lop

This extremely rare lop is characterized by the silver ticking in its very dense coat. In size it is similar to the English Lop, being quite long in the body, without having the bulk of the French Lop. Developed a hundred years ago in eastern Germany, the Meissner is a hardy animal with the ideal coat for the job. Due to the density of its coat, the Meissner is best kept in the cooler parts of the country. Even there it does best if kept outside,

Pet Suitability	✱
Good Points	Temperament, hardy and robust
Poor Points	Very rare – unlikely to find one
Weight	7¾–12¾ lb. (3.5–5.5 kg)
Colors	Black, blue, brown, yellow
Keep In	Pen

Meissner Lop

or it may go into a permanent state of molt.

Perhaps due to the difficulty of getting the coat into show condition in warmer climates, the Meissner Lop has never gained the popularity in Britain that it has in continental Europe. The breed is not recognized by the ARBA.

Holland Lop

The Holland Lop has only been with us since the mid 1990s, but this most endearing of all the breeds has taken the rabbit world by storm. It has certainly become the star of the show.

The inquisitive and sometimes quite comical nature of the Holland Lop can mask its mischievous antics. Like all rabbits, Holland Lops rest through the warmest part of the day, so early mornings and evenings are their playtimes. At these times they are extremely playful. Anything they can find will be turned into a toy to be thrown around and chewed.

Holland Lops love human contact: stroking, petting, cuddling and yes, even kissing. They thrive on it, and these characteristics make them ideal pets for both adults and children.

The Holland Lop is the smallest of the lop

Blue Otter Holland Lop

Black Holland Lop

Holland Lop

breeds, weighing no more than 3½ pounds (1.6 kg). But a good specimen will be a chunky little rabbit with a massive flat-faced head and broad, strong shoulders. It should be short, broad and well muscled with little visible neck. All in all, a good Holland Lop should be a little powerhouse.

In the early days of the breed, malocclusion (distorted teeth) was a serious problem. The chances of it occurring now have been greatly reduced by the care

shown by responsible breeders. But it is still something that should be checked when buying a Holland Lop. If you suspect the teeth are misaligned do not allow your heart to rule your

Agouti Holland Lop

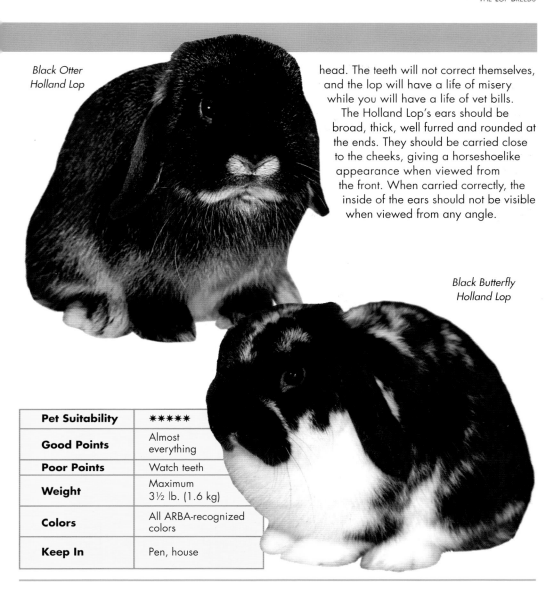

Black Otter Holland Lop

head. The teeth will not correct themselves, and the lop will have a life of misery while you will have a life of vet bills. The Holland Lop's ears should be broad, thick, well furred and rounded at the ends. They should be carried close to the cheeks, giving a horseshoelike appearance when viewed from the front. When carried correctly, the inside of the ears should not be visible when viewed from any angle.

Black Butterfly Holland Lop

Pet Suitability	★★★★★
Good Points	Almost everything
Poor Points	Watch teeth
Weight	Maximum 3½ lb. (1.6 kg)
Colors	All ARBA-recognized colors
Keep In	Pen, house

Sooty Fawn Holland Lop

Seal Point Holland Lop

Orange Holland Lop

Miniature Lion Lop

Young Agouti Lion Lop

Pet Suitability	★★★★
Good Points	Almost everything
Poor Points	Watch teeth
Weight	Maximum 3½ lb. (1.6 kg)
Colors	All ARBA-recognized colors
Keep In	Pen, house

around its body and rump. Because it only has the long hairs around its head it does not present the same grooming problems as the long-haired breeds, such as Angora and Cashmere Lops. Because of this, it is no more difficult to keep in good condition than any other rabbit.

Blue Lion Lop

The Miniature Lion Lop is the newest member of the lop family. It was produced from a cross between the Lionhead and the Holland Lop. With its ancestors being two of today's most popular rabbits, one would expect the Mini Lion Lop to become very popular and for the breed to have a rosy future, but that remains to be seen.

The Miniature Lion Lop has the type and build of the Holland Lop but has a long-haired lion's mane. For exhibition purposes it is considered a fault if the long hairs form a skirt

13 • The Fur Breeds

As the name implies, the fur breeds were bred for their fur. In the Western World there is now very little use made of rabbit fur in the manufacture of garments, but it is less than a hundred years since rabbit fur was used extensively to make some of the finest, and warmest, garments worn by both men and women.

Often called the normal fur breeds, these rabbits have coats of the type that we normally associate with rabbits. They all have strong guard hairs projecting beyond the undercoat (in the wild rabbit these are the black hairs that can readily be seen interspersed among the soft body fur). The normal fur breeds differ from the rex fur breeds in that the latter have shortened guard hairs that should not project beyond the body fur.

With the decline in the use of rabbit fur, the two terms, normal fur breeds and rex fur breeds, have evolved into the fur breeds and the rex breeds, so although you may still hear an old fancier talking about "normals" the term is being used less and less these days.

The fur breeds are much valued for the texture and density of their coats as well as for their individual beauties of color, shading, shape, etc. Many of the fur breeds went to Britain from continental Europe in the decade following the end of the First World War. They were then improved and, in some cases, recreated. Some took the name of the fur-bearing animal that they replicated, such as the Chinchilla, the Sable and the Squirrel.

Opal British Giant

Alaska

The Alaska is a rather thickset, dumpy rabbit that has an intense jet-black coat. The Alaska, which was often called the Nubian in England, is one of the few truly black rabbits and is one of the most beautiful. Black rabbits became extinct in Britain but were reintroduced from Belgium in 1972.

The Alaska was a dual-purpose rabbit, having excellent meat properties as well as a dense, silky and lustrous coat. While its top coat is brilliant black with long and strong guard hairs, it has a deep blue undercoat. Its belly color is also black but matte.

The Alaska was created from a Himalayan x Argent x Dutch cross and was itself used in the creation of the Black Rex. This breed is now so rare in North America that the ARBA has dropped it from its list of recognized breeds.

Pet Suitability	★★★★
Good Points	Size, temperament
Poor Points	Coat will lose color in sunlight
Weight	7–9 lb. (3.2–4 kg)
Colors	Black
Keep In	Pen, cage, house, yard

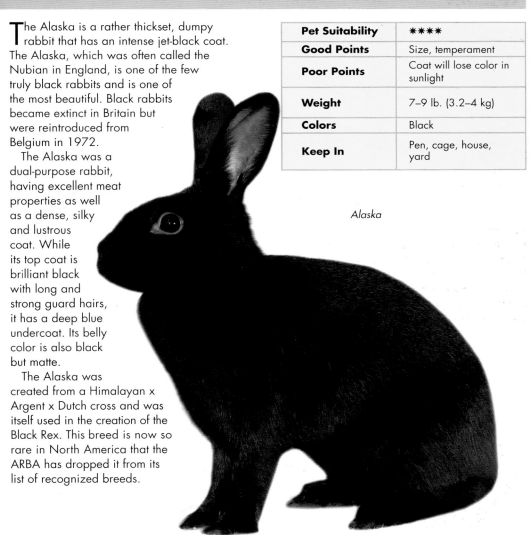

Alaska

157

Argent

The Argent group consists of five differently colored silver rabbits of which only two are recognized by the ARBA. The Champagne d'Argent is one of the oldest known rabbits, having been mentioned in the *Science Encyclopaedia* of 1715. It did not have a formally recognized Standard until 1912 (in France).

All the Argents follow the same pattern. In the nest the coat is a self color. From six to eight weeks they begin to silver, and he process is completed in approximately six to seven months.

Bleu d'Argent

Champagne d'Argent
Approx 8 pounds (3.6 kg)
The Champagne d'Argent is the largest of the Argents; its head is broad and rather long with a round skull, while its body is moderate in length, being neither cobby, nor racy. The Champagne has a dense, silky, glossy coat that lies loose or open rather than close to the body.

The body color is bluish white with a dark slate blue undercoat. The whole of the coat is evenly and moderately interspersed with longer jet-black hairs that give the effect of old silver or pewter when viewed from a distance. It is one of the two breeds recognized by the ARBA (the other is the Creme d'Argent, which is not covered here).

Bleu d'Argent
Approx 6 pounds (2.7 kg)
The Bleu d'Argent is a compact and fairly cobby rabbit that has wide, well-developed hindquarters. Its very dense, glossy, silky coat lies close to the body.

Champagne d'Argent

158

The undercolor is lavender blue, while the body color is bluish white, the whole evenly and moderately interspersed with longer dark blue hairs that give a distinct bluish effect when viewed from a distance.

Brun d'Argent
Approx 6 pounds (2.7 kg)
The Brun is physically identical to the Bleu with the same compact, cobby body.

The undercoat is as deep brown as possible, with the body being a brownish white, the whole evenly and moderately interspersed with longer dark brown hairs that give a distinct brownish effect when viewed from a distance.

Pet Suitability	★★★★
Good Points	Size, temperament
Poor Points	May be difficult to find stock
Weight	See each color
Colors	Brun, bleu, creme, champagne, noir
Keep In	Pen, cage, house, yard

Noir d'Argent

Noir d'Argent
Approx 6 pounds (2.7 kg)
The Noir d'Argent is compact with a fairly cobby body; it has a short neck, broad and rounded loins and wide, well-developed hindquarters. Its short front legs are fine boned. The Noir d'Argent has a very dense, glossy, silky coat that lies close to the body. Its undercolor is deep slate blue with a grayish white body color that is interspersed with longer black guard hairs that give an "old silver" effect when viewed from a distance.

Young Brun d'Argent – still showing self "baby coat" on head.

159

Beveren

The Beveren is a truly utilitarian rabbit, an excellent fur rabbit, a first-rate meat rabbit and a superb showman. They also make wonderful pets. Perhaps the only quarter where it does not excel is as a house rabbit, and that is only because of its intensely dense, silky, lustrous coat, which is between 1 and 1½ inches long (2.5–3.8 cm). A coat like this really does suffer in central heating; it needs to be out in the fresh air, especially in winter when it will thicken up and show its true potential.

The Beveren has a characteristic mandolin shape (as does the English Lop), which gives it a long, broad back with well-developed haunches. It has a bold head with a broad muzzle and long, well-furred ears.

White Beveren

Blue
Perhaps the most popular color. The coat should be light lavender blue, extending to the skin.

White
For the show bench they must be pure white throughout. This color is not easy to keep in this condition if the rabbit is running around the yard, but as long as you do not want to enter any shows it does not really matter if it has stained feet. The whites have blue eyes and are therefore known in the exhibition world as BEWs (blue-eyed whites).

Black
Shortly after the arrival of the Blue Beveren, the black arrived. But it never did become as popular as the blue and therefore did not have the same attention from breeders to develop it. To this day, it is quite unusual to see the lustrous black coat of the black on the show bench.

Brown
During the 1930s breeders developed the Brown Beveren, which is often described as medium brown or nut brown. As with all the Beverens, it is actually the evenness of the color throughout the whole body that is the dominant goal of breeders and exhibitors, rather than the trueness of the actual color.

Pet Suitability	★★★★
Good Points	Size, temperament
Poor Points	Availability
Weight	Not less than 8 lb. (3.6 kg)
Colors	Blue, white, black, brown, lilac
Keep In	Pen, cage, yard

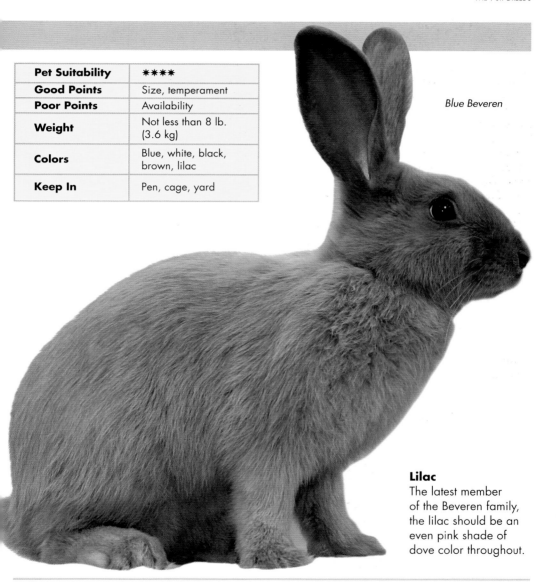

Blue Beveren

Lilac
The latest member of the Beveren family, the lilac should be an even pink shade of dove color throughout.

161

Blanc de Bouscat

The Blanc de Bouscat is a large, long, firm, well-muscled, snow-white rabbit that was bred from crossings between the Champagne d'Argent, the Angora and the Flemish Giant by Madame Dulon of Bouscat in the Gironde region of France in 1906. It was bred as a dual-purpose rabbit; it is an excellent meat rabbit and a prolific breeder. Its litters usually consist of between seven and nine youngsters. The Blanc de Bouscat has a superb snow-white coat that has no pigmentation whatsoever but does have guards hairs sprinkled regularly all over, giving it a brilliant, frosty look.

These are not popular rabbits outside France, and you are unlikely to find one available on the pet market. You would have to seek out a specialist breeder with surplus stock if you did want one.

Pet Suitability	★★★★
Good Points	Size, temperament
Poor Points	Availability
Weight	Not less than 8 lb. (3.6 kg)
Colors	Blue, white, black, brown, lilac
Keep In	Pen, cage, yard

Blanc de Hotot

The exact mix that was used to create the Blanc de Hotot is somewhat unclear, as Baroness Bernhard, the creator, would only admit to using "native French spotted rabbits." The most widely accepted theory is that they were selectively bred using the Giant Papillon Français in combination with other breeds.

Here is another snow-white rabbit that has no pigmentation in its coat, but it differs from the Blanc de Bouscat because it has black eye circles. These resemble fine glasses, which can be considered distinctive or comical depending on your point of view.

The Blanc de Hotot is a somewhat thickset, rounded, compact rabbit with firm musculature and of average size. Its dense, soft, silky fur is said to gleam like frost.

Blanc de Hotot

Pet Suitability	✴✴✴✴
Good Points	Size, temperament
Poor Points	Availability
Weight	8¾–9¾ lb. (4–4.4 kg)
Colors	Snow white except for black eye circles
Keep In	Pen, cage, yard

Blanc de Termonde

Another of the continental snow-white fur/meat utilitarian breeds (this time from Belgium), the Blanc de Termonde is the result of crosses between Flemish Giants and the Beveren Saint Nicholas. With its dense short coat, it is known in continental Europe as a top-quality fur rabbit. Outside Europe it remains a rare breed, and it is seldom seen on the show bench.

Pet Suitability	✴✴✴✴
Good Points	Temperament
Poor Points	Availability
Weight	10–12 lb. (4.5–5.4 kg)
Colors	Snow white
Keep In	Pen, cage, yard

British Giant

This is the largest of the British breeds and can reach up to 20 pounds (9 kg) in weight. They have a large, long, roomy body that is flat on top with broad front and hindquarters. They have a broad, large, full, bold head with erect ears and a bold eye.

The British Giant has a very dense, full coat of ¾–1 inch (2.5–3 cm) in length. British Giants come in six different colors. Whites can have red (REW, or red-eyed white) or blue (BEW, or blue-eyed white) eyes.

Anyone thinking of keeping a rabbit of this size should carefully consider the substantially different costs involved. A big rabbit needs a large pen, which obviously involves an initially higher outlay. There are also the day-to-day running costs, such as the bedding shavings and straw, which will have to be renewed every week of the rabbit's life. Not only will you have to buy a lot of bedding, you will also have to dispose of a lot of fouled bedding. Do you have some way of disposing of a substantial amount of fouled animal bedding?

Some people like little rabbits, but for those who like big ones the British Giant could be just right.

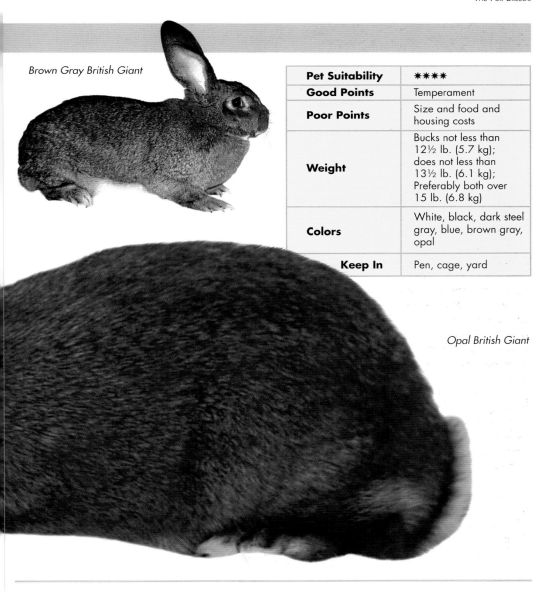

Brown Gray British Giant

Pet Suitability	★★★★
Good Points	Temperament
Poor Points	Size and food and housing costs
Weight	Bucks not less than 12½ lb. (5.7 kg); does not less than 13½ lb. (6.1 kg); Preferably both over 15 lb. (6.8 kg)
Colors	White, black, dark steel gray, blue, brown gray, opal
Keep In	Pen, cage, yard

Opal British Giant

California

Pet Suitability	✳✳✳✳
Good Points	Size, temperament
Poor Points	None
Weight	About 9 lb. (4.1 kg)
Colors	Pure white with colored points in black, chocolate, blue or lilac
Keep In	Pen, cage, yard

Chocolate Californian

As the name suggests, this is a true "Made in the USA" breed. A Mr. West bred it in California. He was a furrier who realized the need for a meat-type rabbit with a good, usable pelt. Originally called the Cochinellas, the name was soon changed to California. In the rabbit world it is affectionately known as the Cali. The Californian was imported into Britain in the 1950s and made its first major show appearance in 1961.

The Californian is a white rabbit with markings which should be as dark as possible (like those of the Himalayan). The markings are, however, the only characteristics similar to the Himalayan, for the Cali is very plump, full over and around the hips with a saddle that should be as meaty as possible to the nape of the neck and down the sides over the ribs and shoulders. Having said all this, they should be very firm and solid and free from over-fatness.

The coat of the Cali is very dense, but it should have enough life to resume its position immediately when rubbed in any direction. It has extremely coarse guard hairs. The points can be black (blacks are known as Normal Californians), chocolate, blue or lilac.

Chinchilla

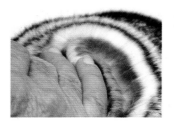

LEFT
Chinchilla banding

RIGHT
Chinchilla

The Standard Chinchilla has been described as the fur rabbit par excellence. In the days when furriers sought rabbit pelts to make into clothing, it was the Chinchilla's pelt that was the most highly prized. The Chinchilla rabbit was originally bred in France to imitate the *Chinchilla lanigera*, the little fur-bearing rodent from the Andes, but the quality of its fur has probably surpassed that of the South American animal.

The Chinchilla (or Chin, as it is more often referred to) was first imported into Britain in 1919 and very quickly gained an enormous following among rabbit breeders. It should be remembered that the 1920s and 30s were times of extreme financial difficulty for many people in Britain, and here was a rabbit that would not only feed the family with high-protein meat, but whose pelt was much sought after and fetched very high prices. There can be little wonder that the Chin became so popular.

The Chin remains a popular exhibition rabbit among lovers of the fur breeds because of the intricacy of its coloring. If you part the fur with the edge of your hand you will see an undercolor of dark slate blue at the base with a clearly defined pearly white intermediate portion edged with a narrow black line and surmounted with gray fur brightly ticked with black hairs. The coat is exquisitely soft, fine and dense and between 1 and 1½ inches (3–4 cm) in length.

Chinchillas are quite hardy and will happily spend their lives outside. The does make excellent mothers and are good tempered. The central heating in modern houses will prevent the Chinchilla's coat from ever really achieving its glorious best, so they are far better being kept outside where their coats can bloom.

Pet Suitability	★★★★
Good Points	Size, temperament
Poor Points	Dense coat (heavy molter)
Weight	About 7 lb. (3.2 kg)
Colors	To resemble real Chinchilla
Keep In	Pen, cage, yard

Giant Chinchilla

It would be easy to say that the Giant Chinchilla is just a giant version of the Chinchilla, but this is not quite true. Certainly it is a much larger rabbit, but the surface of the coat is a mixture of bright blue and silver tippings interspersed with longer black-tipped guard hairs. This combination gives a "mackerel" effect to the coat while making it a considerably darker gray than the Chinchilla rabbit.

As the name suggests this is a big rabbit; anyone considering sharing their lives with one of these giants should be aware that they are not cuddly little bunnies and can be quite strong willed and determined. Having said that, if they suit your lifestyle and circumstances you will be greatly rewarded with much love and attention from a devoted pet.

Pet Suitability	★★★★
Good Points	Temperament
Poor Points	Size, dense coat (heavy molter), availability
Weight	About 12 lb. (5.4 kg)
Colors	Darker gray than the Chinchilla
Keep In	Pen, cage, yard

Continental Giant

If you are the kind of person who likes Great Danes or Saint Bernard dogs, then this could be just the rabbit for you. The Conti (as it is always called) is above all big. It is a massive, solid-looking rabbit that gives an overall impression of power. The body of the Conti should be at least 25 inches (65 cm) long, and its ears should be approximately one quarter the length of its body. So the Continental Giant is a very big rabbit with very big upright ears.

Pet Suitability	★★★★
Good Points	Temperament
Poor Points	Size and food and housing costs
Weight	Up to 20 lb. (9 kg)
Colors	Black, dark steel, light steel, agouti, opal yellow
Keep In	Pen, cage, yard

The Continental Giant is much bigger than the British Giant and the Giant Chinchilla. In fact, it is bigger than all the other giants.

If you are tempted to take on a Conti as a companion, you will need a pen that is at least 6 feet long by 3 feet high (2 m x 1 m). Preferably it should be much bigger and have a huge run attached to it so this gentle giant can exercise properly. They need to be in contact with a variety of stimulations that will keep them interested and active and prevent them from becoming lazy and fat.

Agouti Continental Giant

170

Deilenaar

The Deilenaar hails from Holland and is quite a rare rabbit outside its homeland. It is very handsome, short and thickset and is a well-rounded, mid-sized rabbit. It was created from the Belgian Hare, the New Zealand Red and the Chinchilla, which would account for the top color resembling that of a Hare – a warm reddish brown with strong, wavy ticking.

The Deilenaar has not really caught on in North America and you would almost certainly have to look long and hard to find one that was for sale.

Pet Suitability	★★★★
Good Points	Size, temperament
Poor Points	Quite difficult to find
Weight	About 7½ lb. (3.2 kg)
Colors	Warm red/brown
Keep In	Pen, cage, yard

Fauve de Bourgogne

Pet Suitability	★★★
Good Points	Size, temperament
Poor Points	Extremely rare, very difficult to find
Weight	9–11 lb. (4–5 kg)
Colors	Yellow/red
Keep In	Pen, cage, yard

The French-created Fauve de Bourgogne only arrived in Britain in 2005, making it one of the newest breeds to be accepted by the British Rabbit Council's Breeds Standards Committee. It is not recognized by the ARBA.

Everything about this rabbit says strong; the body is stocky, massive and well rounded, and the front and rear widths are equal. The neck is short and strong. The front legs are strong and of medium length. The head is strong with a broad forehead. The ears are strong, standing firm and erect. This may only be a medium-sized rabbit, but it is most definitely a robust animal.

The top color of the Fauve is said to be a uniform yellow/red, which stretches evenly over the whole body. The fur on this super rabbit is medium in length, but it does have a very dense undercoat, which means that it would not be ideal as a house rabbit, as it would be unlikely to achieve its beautiful coat if kept in a centrally heated house.

The Fauve is quite a popular rabbit in France and even has two specialist breed clubs; unfortunately it will likely be quite difficult to get hold of stock in North America.

Silver Fox

The Silver Fox was created in Britain in the 1920s, and bred to imitate the wild silver fox. Since then it has grown in popularity in the rabbit exhibition world. However, limited stock in North America means most breeders have rather long waiting lists, so pet stock is not easy to come by. The breed is far more common in Britain, where pet stock is relatively easy to find.

In the early days of breeding the Chinchilla, it was not unusual for a black rabbit with a white belly to turn up in a litter. It was the usual practice to destroy these odd-colored youngsters to give the looked-for Chinchillas a better chance. But when one of these black youngsters was allowed to grow up, it was found to be a beautiful black rabbit resembling a silver fox. With its jet-black coat, white underparts and profuse sprinkling of longer white hairs along its flanks and chest, it was indeed an object of great splendor. It was found that when two of these black rabbits were mated together they bred true. The rest, as they say, is history.

Black Silver Fox

Pet Suitability	★★★★★
Good Points	Size, temperament
Poor Points	Maintaining the beautiful lustrous coat, availability
Weight	About 7½ lb. (3.2 kg)
Colors	Black, blue, chocolate, lilac
Keep In	Pen, cage, yard

Blue Silver Fox

The gleaming jet-black coat with its protruding white hairs contrasting so vividly with the snow-white underneath has made the Silver Fox popular in the show world. And, as it is a hardy, robust rabbit of average size, it is also a suitable pet.

The Silver Fox now comes in black, blue, chocolate and lilac, and the breed has also been "dwarfed" (as the Netherland Dwarf), "lopped" (as the Mini and Holland Lops), and even "rexed" (as the tan-patterned Rex).

Chocolate Silver Fox

173

Havana

The medium-sized Havana will naturally appeal to many because it does not need the large pen or have the increased overheads of the larger rabbit breeds. This compact little rabbit was developed in Holland. It spread throughout Europe in the early 1900s and was recognized by the ARBA as a breed in 1916.

The Blue Havana was developed in the United States and, along with the black, broken and chocolate, is recognized as a breed. However, in Britain the Havana comes

Pet Suitability	✶✶✶✶✶
Good Points	Size, availability
Poor Points	Temperament can occasionally be a bit suspect
Weight	About 5½–6½ lb. (2.5–2.9 kg)
Colors	Blue, black, chocolate, broken
Keep In	Pen, cage, yard

in only one color, a rich, dark chocolate with a purplish sheen.

Although the Havana is a popular exhibition rabbit in its own right, it is its use in crossing-in its distinctive chocolate color to other breeds that has really established its importance.

Havana

Lilac

Essex Lavender, Cambridge Lilac and Cambridge Blue are just some of the earlier names that were used for what we now call the Lilac. Crossing the chocolate-colored Havana with the Blue Beveren produced the Lilac, which has a dove-gray fur that is soft, exquisitely silky and intensely dense. Like the Havana, the Lilac is compact, well fleshed and fine boned.

The Lilac is not particularly popular today, and you will have difficulty finding stock.

Pet Suitability	★★★★
Good Points	Size, temperament
Poor Points	Availability
Weight	About 5½–7 lb. (2.5–3.2 kg)
Colors	Pinkish shade of dove
Keep In	Pen, cage, yard

Lilac

New Zealand White

Probably the rabbit with the highest worldwide population, the New Zealand White is the archetypal "meat rabbit" and is extremely popular wherever commercial rabbit farming is practiced. Contrary to its name, this is an American-bred rabbit that was kept by the thousand at the height of the American commercial rabbit trade. It is said that a well-fed litter of New Zealand Whites would attain a live weight of 4 pounds (1.8 kg) each at just eight weeks old, and this was without reducing the litter size.

Fairly long in the body, it would be difficult to find a rabbit carrying more flesh on its hind legs. Its broad back is almost as wide at the shoulders as at the hindquarters. This was a truly dual-purpose rabbit. Furriers loved its pure white pelt, which, unlike colored pelts, could easily be dyed to any color, even the subtlest of

Pet Suitability	★★★★★
Good Points	Availability, temperament
Poor Points	Size
Weight	About 11 lb. (5 kg)
Colors	Bright clean white
Keep In	Pen, cage, yard

pastel shades. Its coat is very dense and thick to the touch, and is neither too fine and silky nor harsh and wiry.

The New Zealand continues to be popular in the U.S., and both blue and broken varieties are being developed.

New Zealand White

New Zealand Red

Pet Suitability	★★★★
Good Points	Size, temperament
Poor Points	Availability
Weight	About 8 lb. (3.6 kg)
Colors	Bright golden red
Keep In	Pen, cage, yard

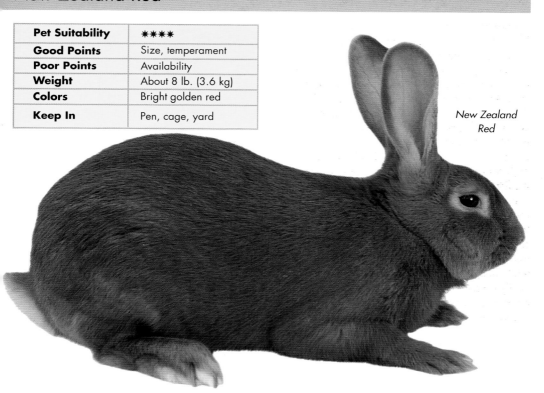

New Zealand Red

Like the New Zealand White, the New Zealand Red originated in the U.S. and is the oldest of the New Zealand breeds. At only 8 pounds (3.6 kg) in weight, the Red is considerably smaller than the New Zealand White and has a markedly different coat. Its bright golden red coat (sometimes described as reddish gold with sheen) is dense and quite harsh in texture and only ¾ inch (2 cm) in length. All the other fur breeds have fur that is at least 1 inch (3 cm) in length, which lies close to the skin and has plenty of guard hairs.

The New Zealand is also available in black, which is only rarely found in Britain but is more common in North America.

177

Perlfee

Perlfee

The Perlfee is little known, even in its German homeland. A fairly small, cobby rabbit that is fine boned, it has an almost invisible neck. It was bred in imitation of the Siberian squirrel.

The Perlfee's grayish blue coat comes in three shades: light, medium and dark. Exhibitors prefer the medium shade. The tips of the guard hairs are light gray and dark gray, and it is this coloring that gives its coat a distinctive blue gray pearled reflection.

The Perlfee is a very rare rabbit that is unlikely to come onto the pet market.

Pet Suitability	✳✳✳
Good Points	Size, temperament
Poor Points	Availability
Weight	About 5½–8 lb. (2.4–3.7 kg)
Colors	Grayish blue
Keep In	Pen, cage, yard

Rhinelander

The Rhinelander is a medium-sized rabbit, which, as the name suggests, originates from Germany. The Rhinelander is one of the few tri-color breeds; it is white with black and yellow makings. As with so many of the similarly marked rabbits, it is a breeder's nightmare. The challenge of getting the spots the right size in the right place and of the right color is one that few breeders are prepared to take on. The result is that the Rhinelander is quite a rare breed, and, unless you happen to have a breeder living near you, you are unlikely to see them other than at the big shows.

The Rhinelander is a thickset rabbit that is quite rounded, being the same width from front to back. It is a well-proportioned, weight-to-size rabbit that has a dense and silky coat that is not too long.

Pet Suitability	✽✽✽✽
Good Points	Size, temperament
Poor Points	Rare and difficult to find
Weight	6–9 lb. (2.7–4.4 kg)
Colors	White base with black and yellow markings
Keep In	Pen, cage, house, yard

Rhinelander

Sable

There are two types of Sables: the Marten, which has a white belly and ticking along the flanks exactly the same as the Fox pattern, and the Siamese, which has a dark belly and no ticking. Both of them can be bred together and a proportion of each type will be represented in the resulting litter.

The Sables are another breed that owes at least a part of its genetic inheritance to the Chinchilla. Beautiful brown-shaded youngsters appeared in Chinchilla litters. When these animals were bred from they turned out to breed true, with pelts that resembled those of the wild sable. Both the Marten and the Siamese come in three shades: light, medium and dark. It was the medium that was originally

Siamese Sable

Medium Marten Sable

favored by the exhibitors, and many perfectly good light and dark youngsters were discarded purely because they were the wrong shade. But eventually classes were introduced for each of the three shades.

Medium-sized, neat, cobby rabbit, with a moderate length of body, Sables make ideal pets. They live happily in average-sized pens. They have amiable, easy-going natures and are very undemanding rabbits but respond well to lots of love and attention.

Pet Suitability	★★★★
Good Points	Size, temperament
Poor Points	None
Weight	About 5–7 lb. (2.3–3.2 kg)
Colors	Rich sepia
Keep In	Pen, cage, yard

Sallander

Bred in the Netherlands, the Sallander is the outcome of crosses between the Thuringer, the Chinchilla and the Marten Sable. This produced a thickset, well-rounded rabbit with very dense, silky fur that should feel very soft to the touch.

The base color of the Sallander is a light cinnamon or pearl, while the tips of the guard hairs are brownish black. This gives an overall "hazed" appearance that creates a veil of pale charcoal-colored fur.

The Sallander is quite an unusual rabbit, and it would be difficult to find one for sale as a pet, as there are few of them around.

LEFT: Sallander

Pet Suitability	✱✱✱
Good Points	Size, temperament
Poor Points	Availability
Weight	5¾–9½ lb. (2.5–4.3 kg)
Colors	Pearl with a veil or haze of pale charcoal
Keep In	Pen, cage, yard

Satin

Pet Suitability	✶✶✶✶
Good Points	Size, temperament, availability
Poor Points	None
Weight	6–8 lb. (2.7–3.6 kg)
Colors	All self colors
Keep In	Pen, cage, yard

The satin coat was a mutation that appeared in a litter of Chocolate Havanas in the United States during the 1930s. The satin factor is a recessive characteristic. Despite this, and like the rex gene, the satin gene has now been bred into a large number of breeds. We now have satin counterparts for most rabbit breeds. The original Satin rabbits were mostly ivories with pink eyes.

The Satin's coat is quite unique. It has an exquisitely smooth, silky, satinlike texture and sheen. It is, perhaps, the lustrous sheen that separates its coat from all others. In the United States and continental Europe, the "satinizing" of coats in all breeds is well advanced.

Ivory Satin

Siberian

The Siberian is another of the medium-sized fur rabbits with a wonderful coat. Nobody is quite sure why it was called the Siberian because it is actually a true English creation. Mr. Banfield, an Essex breeder, created the breed in 1930 when trying to produce a rabbit specifically for small farms, which would deliver a high-quality pelt. He certainly succeeded, because the coat is the outstanding feature of the breed. It is believed that self-colored English and Havana animals were used to produce the original coffee-colored brown rabbit. Later, blacks, blues and lilacs were added.

The coat of the Siberian (usually abbreviated to the "Sib" in the rabbit world) should be roll-back or blanket fur and when turned in the reverse direction should give the impression of having been sheared or pulled to expose as few guard hairs as possible. The result is a neat

Brown Siberian

rabbit of medium size with a moderate length of body, medium-boned feet and legs and a very dense, glossy fur with an exquisite texture.

With the demise of the rabbit fur trade, the Sib, like so many of the fur rabbits, is now, unfortunately, becoming less common and may be difficult to obtain.

Pet Suitability	✹✹✹✹✹
Good Points	Size, temperament
Poor Points	Availability
Weight	5–7 lb. (2.3–3.2 kg)
Colors	Black, blue, brown, lilac
Keep In	Pen, cage, yard

Young Blue Siberian

Smoke Pearl

Pet Suitability	★★★★★
Good Points	Size, temperament
Poor Points	Availability
Weight	5–7 lb. (2.3–3.2 kg)
Colors	Smoke – marten type or siamese type
Keep In	Pen, cage, yard

Smoke Pearl

Originally known as the Smoke Beige, the Smoke Pearl is often described as the Sable dressed in gray. Just like the Sable, the Smoke Pearl comes in the marten type, with the chest, flanks, rump and feet well ticked with long white hairs and the belly and underside white, and also in the siamese type. The overall effect of both types is the smoke appearance.

The Smoke Pearl has, as you would expect for a fur rabbit, a superb coat. It is soft and very dense with an under fur that is exquisitely silky and exceedingly full and dense.

If you can find one, a Smoke Pearl would make a super little pet that should, for the sake of its dense coat, best be kept outside.

Sussex

The Sussex comes in two varieties, the Sussex Cream and the Sussex Gold. The difference between the two is, as the names suggest, in the color. The Gold has a cream undercolor, deepening evenly to a red gold top color, which is lightly ticked with cream. The shadings are described as light milk chocolate and the rabbit's eyes are reddish brown. The Cream Sussex has a pale cream undercolor, deepening evenly to a rich pinkish cream color, which is lightly ticked with lilac and lilac shadings. The eyes of the Cream are lilac gray.

The Sussex is a compact, cobby medium-sized rabbit with a broad chest and well-muscled shoulders; its coat is very dense and silky with strong guard hairs.

Even if you are lucky enough to find a breeder of Sussex rabbits – and there are very few of them – you will probably have to wait some time for one to become available. But your wait will be rewarded. The Sussex is an absolutely charming rabbit that will make anyone a super companion.

Pet Suitability	★★★★
Good Points	Size, temperament
Poor Points	Availability – they are quite rare
Weight	7½ lb. (3.4 kg)
Colors	Reddish tortoiseshell with either brown or lilac shadings
Keep In	Pen, cage, yard

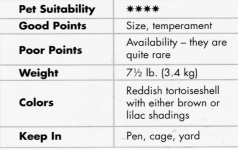

Sussex Cream

Swiss Fox

The Swiss Fox is very different to all the other fur rabbits in that it is long haired. The fur length of the Swiss Fox should be no longer than 2¾ inches (7 cm) and no shorter

Black Swiss Fox

Pet Suitability	✱✱
Good Points	Size, temperament
Poor Points	Availability
Weight	5½–8¾ lb. (2.5–4 kg)
Colors	All recognized colors
Keep In	Pen, cage

than 1¾ inches (4.6 cm). Although most of the fur rabbits have fur shorter than 1½ inches (4 cm), there are noticeable differences in the fur length of various breeds in this category. Swiss Fox fur is slightly longer than that of the Cashmere Lop, but not quite as long as that of the Angora. The long coat is a factor that should be given careful consideration, as this breed needs grooming on a regular basis. For example, the Swiss Fox should not really be left to roam free in a yard where it can entangle foreign bodies in its coat.

But if you are prepared to keep the Swiss Fox as a pen rabbit, you can have a medium to large rabbit with a strong, vigorous, well-rounded body that can make a wonderful pet.

*Blue-eyed White
Swiss Fox*

Thuringer

Thuringer

As the name suggests, the Thuringer originates from the Province of Thuringia in Germany, where a schoolmaster who crossed Himalayans, Argents and giant rabbits created it.

The Thuringer is a thickset, well-rounded rabbit with a very dense, close, short and lustrous coat. The general color is a yellow ocher or buff (chamois leather), but the guard hairs are bluish black in color, which produces a haze of pale charcoal. To this haze effect is added a shaded pattern in sooty (or charcoal). These sooty shadings extend over the nose, ears, chest, lower half of the shoulders, flanks, rump, top of the tail, legs and belly.

The Thuringer is a very attractive rabbit that would make an ideal pet for the house or yard. However, there are only a few of them around, so you could well be in for a bit of a hunt to find one.

Pet Suitability	★★★★
Good Points	Size, temperament
Poor Points	Availability
Weight	5¾–9½ lb. (2.5–4.3 kg)
Colors	Yellow ocher with a haze of pale charcoal
Keep In	Pen, cage, house, yard

Vienna

Strictly speaking, the Vienna Blue, Vienna White and Vienna Black are three different breeds. Just over 100 years ago they were quite different from one another. The White was considerably smaller than the Blue, for example. But in recent years the three breeds have converged to the point where all three rabbits are exactly the same, other than for the color.

The Viennas are thickset, well-muscled rabbits. While they are not as big as the giants, everything about them exudes strength, and they are powerful.

Pet Suitability	★★★★
Good Points	Temperament
Poor Points	Size, availability
Weight	About 7–12 lb. (3.5–5.4 kg)
Colors	Blue: dark slate blue; white: white with blue eyes; black: jet black
Keep In	Pen, cage, yard

The Vienna Blues are a dark slate blue, which should be uniform over the entire body and very lustrous. Their fur is exquisitely dense, silky and rich in guard hairs. The Vienna Whites must be

a uniform pure white over the entire body and very lustrous. The White also has the same exquisitely dense, silky coat as the Blue. Similarly, the Vienna Black must be jet-black.

The Blues have always been more popular than the Whites, and the Blacks are now quite rare. The sight of a quality Vienna Blue in top show condition is a spectacle to behold. But like all the fur rabbits, it is more about "feel" than looks, and you really have to run your hands through the coat to appreciate the extraordinary quality of a Vienna Blue in top condition.

The Viennas have declined in popularity in recent years, in line with all of the fur rabbits. There is no longer any market for their pelts, and they are big rabbits that need big pens and a lot of food. But if you do feel that you have the time, energy and money to keep a Vienna, they are wonderful rabbits that will return all the love and attention that you give them twice over.

The ARBA does not recognize any vienna breeds.

Vienna White

Rare Breeds

Some of the breeds that have now become so rare that you are unlikely to find them:

Golden Glavcot

Hulstlander

Pointed Beveren

Beige

Wheaten

Lynx (Wheaten)

Squirrel

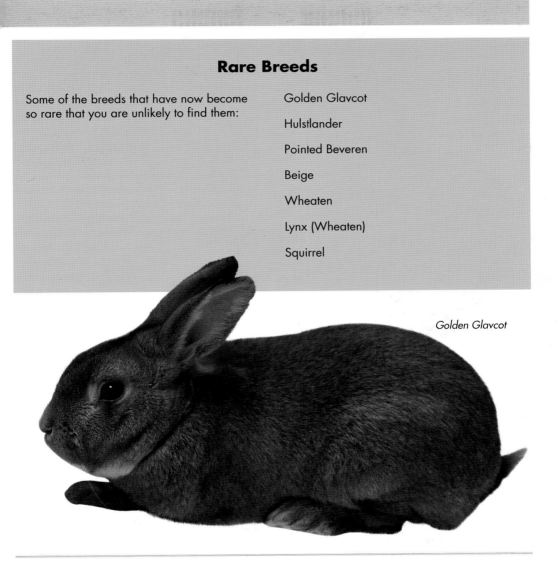

Golden Glavcot

14 • The Rex Breeds

It is the coat of the rex rabbits that distinguishes them from all other breeds of rabbit. Rex rabbits have an intensely dense, smooth, firm, plush, velvetlike coat devoid of guard hairs (the coarser hairs of greater length than the body hairs that are quite normal to all breeds of rabbit).

In recent years breeders have developed a smaller version of the traditional rex rabbit so that we now have two sizes, the Mini Rex and the Standard Rex. Both come in mostly the same varieties, although some varieties that are accepted in the Mini are not accepted in the Standard and vice versa; the only other difference should be that the Mini Rex is about half the size of the Standard Rex.

MINI REX	3½–4½ lb. (1.6–2 kg)
STANDARD REX	6–8 lb. (2.7–3.6 kg)

Although rex rabbits come in all recognized colors, it is white (also known as ermine) and black that are by far the most popular in the exhibition world. It is quite common for the rex to take top honors at major shows. Because of the need to keep the show specimens spotlessly clean and to prevent the sun from affecting the coloring of their coats, "show" rexes are always kept in an indoor rabbitry. However, their robust, amenable nature makes them ideal pets. So long as they have a warm, dry, draft-free pen to sleep in, they are more than happy to spend their lives running around the yard, and they make excellent companion rabbits.

Unlike most other breeds of rabbit, which were developed by deliberately crossing two breeds that carried desired characteristics, the rex was a genetic mutation that appeared spontaneously.

It was 1919, in the farmyard of Désiré Caillon in the Sarthe District of France, that this strange "mutation" was first seen: a rabbit minus any guard hairs. Mr. Caillon showed this odd rabbit to the local parish priest, the Abbot Gillet. The abbot verified that this was indeed a very different breed, and he named it Castorrex – king of the beavers. He then began breeding them. However, the abbot had no knowledge of genetics, and all his stock from the farmer was so inbred that the offspring were sickly animals that did not prosper.

As in all good stories with happy endings, a wise man in the shape of the president of the French Agricultural Society, Mr. Wiltzer, went to see the abbot's Castorrex rabbits. It was Wiltzer who identified the inbreeding problem and recommended that the solution was to bring in an outcross.

In 1925 the story continues with Professor Kohler, who bought three Castorrex and crossed them with white, black, fawn and chinchilla rabbits. In 1926 he was able to show Ermine Rex, Black Rex and Chinchilla Rex. Professor Kohler published his method in 1927. In mating Castorrex bucks to does of all the existing breeds, he was able to fix to the essential characteristics in which he was interested: color and the absence of guard hairs.

The first rexes were exported to Britain and the United States in the mid-1920s, but they were extremely ugly, ungainly rabbits with oversized ears – the British often called them "wrecks." Breeders have improved the rex type beyond all recognition, and the heavily plushed coat we see today is a result of all their hard work.

Otter Rex

195

Self Rex

Black Along with the White Rex, the coat of the Black Rex has been perfected by breeders to an incredibly high standard; the consequence of this is that these two colors of rex frequently claim the highest honors at even the biggest shows. The coat of the Black Rex is a rich, lustrous blue black with a dark blue undercoat carried right down to the skin.

White The coat of a top-quality show White Rex is something to behold. Half an inch (1.3 cm) in depth, the fine silky texture must be free of any harshness or woolliness. It will be intensely dense, smooth and level over the whole body.
Needless to say, an exhibition White Rex will be spotlessly clean. Yes, they really do have white feet.

Blue Perhaps because of the difficulty in maintaining the clear, bright medium shade of blue, which should not tend to lavender, the Blue Rex has never been as popular as the Black or White. Maybe because of this difficulty in getting the color right, it is not uncommon for those that do not quite come up to standard to be sold as pets, for which their amenable temperament is ideally suited.

White Rex

Pet Suitability	★★★★★	
Good Points	Hardy, temperament	
Poor Points	Coat will lose color in sun	
Weight	Mini Rex	3½ –4½ lb. (1.6–2 kg)
	Standard Rex	6–8 lb. (2.7–3.6 kg)
Colors	Black, white, blue, chocolate, lilac, nutria	
Keep In	Pen, cage, house, yard	

Blue Rex

Chocolate Also known as the Havana Rex, the Chocolate Rex is (or should be) a rich, dark chocolate color. If you use the edge of your hand to separate the coat, you will see that the chocolate color goes far down the hair shaft, and then there is a pearl gray undercolor next to the skin. The Chocolate Rex has eyes the same color as its coat, but they will glow ruby red in subdued light.

Lilac The Lilac is not a very popular color of rex; its pinkish dove gray color is often mistaken for a poorly colored Blue.

Nutria Even more rare than the Lilac, the Nutria Rex has a rich golden brown coat and is extremely unusual.

Black Rex

Chocolate Rex

197

Shaded Rex

Smoke Pearl The shaded rex breeds are characterized by having a darker saddle from nape to tail that shades off to a lighter color on the flanks. The Smoke Pearl has a smoke gray saddle that shades to pearl gray on the flanks, chest and belly. From an exhibitor's point of view the shading must be gradual, avoiding blotches and streaks. The Smoke Pearl Rex also has the ruby red glow to its eye when seen in a subdued light.

Sable Siamese The saddle of the Sable Siamese Rex is rich sepia brown, shading gradually to a chestnut on the flanks and

slightly paler on the belly. Like the other shaded **rex breeds, the Sable Siamese has the ruby red glow to its eyes when viewed in subdued lighting.**

Seal Rex

Seal The Seal has an even, rich, dark sepia head and body; the shading is only slightly paler on the lower flanks, chest and belly. The ruby red eye is again present.

Smoke Pearl Rex

Tortoiseshell The tortoiseshell color in rabbits is variously known as tort, Madagascar or sooty fawn depending on the specific breed. In rexes the color is always called tortoiseshell, although this color is not recognized by the ARBA. The top color (or saddle) is a rich orange lightly tipped with brown; the ears, muzzle, feet, belly and underside of the tail are a rich blue black that gradually shades into the body color on the face, flanks and haunches.

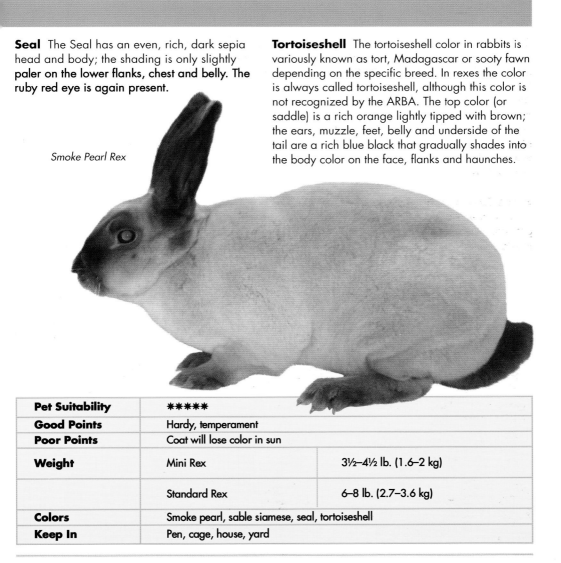

Pet Suitability	★★★★★	
Good Points	Hardy, temperament	
Poor Points	Coat will lose color in sun	
Weight	Mini Rex	3½–4½ lb. (1.6–2 kg)
	Standard Rex	6–8 lb. (2.7–3.6 kg)
Colors	Smoke pearl, sable siamese, seal, tortoiseshell	
Keep In	Pen, cage, house, yard	

Tan Pattern Rex

Tan pattern rex rabbits are all characterized by the distinctive markings that they have inherited from the original Black Tan rabbit (see pages 137–138). Perhaps the most easily identified feature of the tan pattern is the nape triangle, which is usually white or tan depending on the breed. It appears directly behind the ears, where it is at its broadest. The triangle narrows to a point at the rear. In the actual Tan rabbit the triangle runs into a kind of collar that encircles the neck. This is not the case in the tan-patterned rex breeds, where it simply forms the nape triangle.

Other features of the tan pattern are the ring of color around each eye known as the eye circles. The nostrils, jowl, chest, belly, flanks and the underpart of the tail will pick up the same color as the eye circles, which is usually tan or white.

Marten Sable The Martin Sable Rex's saddle is an even, rich sepia brown, shading gradually to a rich chestnut on the flanks. The nape triangle and other markings are white.

Marten Seal The Seal Rex, which is a shaded rex, is a beautiful, rich, dark sepia that only shades slightly paler to its lower flanks, chest and belly. The Marten Seal (which is a tan-patterned rex) has the same beautiful, rich, dark sepia coloring, but it has a white belly, eye circles, inside of the ears, underside of the jowl and nape triangle.

Fawn Rex

Pet Suitability	★★★★★	
Good Points	Hardy, temperament	
Poor Points	Coat will lose color in sun	
Weight	Mini Rex	3½–4½ lb. (1.6– 2 kg)
	Standard Rex	6–8 lb. (2.7–3.6 kg)
Colors	Marten sable; marten seal; red; fawn; fox in black, blue, chocolate, lilac; otter in black, blue, chocolate, lilac; tan in black, blue, chocolate, lilac	
Keep In	Pen, cage, house, yard	

Tan Rex

flanks and rump, which are inherited features from the Silver Fox.

Otter The otter pattern is characterized by the distinct border of tan coloring that divides the top color (black, blue, chocolate or lilac) from the creamy white of the belly, underside of the chin and tail.

Tan The Tan Rex is as near its ancestral parent in color as possible, with its belly, chest, eye circles, inside of its ears, underside of its jowls and nape triangle a beautiful, rich tan color that contrasts with its top color, which can be black, blue, chocolate or lilac.

Red The Red Rex is a truly stunning deep, rich orange color that gradually shades to a white belly. Eye circles, inside of the ears and the underside of the jowl are all white. The Red Rex does not have a discernable nape triangle.

Fawn The Fawn Rex is a bright golden fawn that has no trace of creaminess. It has a white belly, eye circles, inside of the ears, underside of the jowl and nape triangle.

Fox The fox pattern (black, blue, chocolate or lilac) is characterized by the white ticking on the

Otter Rex

Red Rex

201

Agouti Pattern Rex

Agouti is the color of the wild rabbit, and the agouti pattern takes its name from the similarities with the coat pattern of the wild rabbit. If a hand is used to separate the agouti-patterned rabbit's coat, so that you can see the depth of fur right down to the skin, the fur will be banded. In the Castor Rex the fur will be a dark, rich chestnut at the top with a band of rich orange clearly defined from the dark slate blue undercoat.

All agouti-patterned rabbits have this characteristic banding, with the colors of the individual bands varying for each color of rabbit.

Lynx Rex

Castor Rex The Castor Rex (Castorrex) was the original rex rabbit that the Abbot Gillet bred in France. All subsequent Rexes have been bred from the Castorrex. While the Castors have lost out in the popularity stakes to the Brokens, Blacks and Whites in recent years, the sight of an in-coat Castor

Adult Castor Rex showing banding.

Rex, with its rich chestnut top coat and contrasting white belly and underside of the tail, is a magnificent spectacle.

Chinchilla It would be to easy to describe the Chinchilla Rex (also called Chinrex) as just a gray rabbit, but it is the sparkling chinchillated effect of the black- and white-tipped fur that characterizes this magnificent rabbit. The banding on the Chinchilla Rex is dark slate blue at the base, followed by a band of white below the black and white tips.

Cinnamon The coat of the Cinnamon Rex is a bright golden tan on the top with a band of light orange below with a blue/gray undercoat.

Lynx The Lynx is probably the least common of the agouti-patterned Rexes and is rarely seen. But its orange coat shot through with silver is quite unique. The Lynx has a bright

Pet Suitability	★★★★★	
Good Points	Hardy, temperament	
Poor Points	Coat will lose color in sun	
Weight	Mini Rex	3½–4½ lb. (1.6–2 kg)
	Standard Rex	6–8 lb. (2.7–3.6 kg)
Colors	Castor, chinchilla, cinnamon, lynx, opal, amber	
Keep In	Pen, cage, house, yard	

Chinchilla Rex

orange band in
its coat that is
clearly defined from
its white undercoat.

Opal In some of the lop
breeds the blue agouti or opal is
a very popular color. However, few breeders
have decided to specialize in this less common
color. The Opal's topcoat is a pale shade of
blue and there is a layer of golden tan between
it and the slate blue undercolor. The overall
effect is of blue shot with tan.

Other Varieties of Rex

Over the years, successive generations of rabbit fanciers have sought to breed almost every pattern and color of rabbit into the rex. As we have seen, many have been very successful. But sometimes, despite a lifetime's work in perfecting a new color or pattern into the rex, the final article does not catch on with other fanciers. It is these "other varieties" that come into this class.

Having said that, the Broken Rex is not at all rare – it is the most popular rex in the United States and is the most commonly found variety at ARBA-sponsored shows.

The next main patterns in this class are not rare, but neither are they common. The Dalmation Rex, the Harlequin/Magpie Rex, the Himalayan Rex and the Tri-Color Rex are all exact copies of their parent breed, and one should refer to the notes on the originating **breed for guidance on the pattern and color.**

Astrex White

To these "other varieties" we can add two more, but these are so rare that they may well not even still exist.

Otter Mini Rex

Tri Dali

Broken Mini Rex

The Silver Seal Rex has a jet-black coat that has an even silvering all over, giving it a sparkling effect.

The Satin Rex can be in any recognized color or pattern of rex, but the coat has been "satinized." That is to say the coat has a fine satinlike texture and distinctive sheen.

The Rough-Coated Rex

Even rarer than any of the previously discussed rex colors and patterns are the two Rough-Coated Rex breeds, the Astrex and the Opossum. Both are so exceptionally uncommon that it is probably fairly safe to say that neither actually exists anymore.

Himalayan Rex

Pet Suitability	★★★★★	
Good Points	Hardy, temperament	
Poor Points	Coat will lose color in sun, availability of some varieties	
Weight	Mini Rex	3½–4½ lb. (1.6–2 kg)
	Standard Rex	6–8 lb. (2.7–3.6 kg)
Colors	Dalmation, harlequin/magpie, Himalayan, tri-color, broken, Californian	
Keep In	Pen, cage, house, yard	

Index

Acknowledgments

Pat Gaskin: *Fur & Feather* magazine; Lisa Kelsall for use of the picture of Dylan, her Rhinelander rabbit; Emma Magnu